ANGLIAN ANNALS

More moments in time in eastern England

PETER SARGENT

Also by **Peter Sargent**

A Moment in Time (2017)
A Place in History (2018)

_____

Catch up with Peter Sargent's
latest news, books and blog at
www.petersargent.co.uk

ANGLIAN ANNALS

More moments in time in eastern England

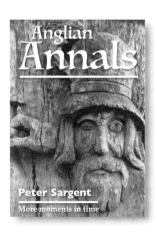

Cover picture is a close-up of Mark Goldsworthy's sculpture depicting Elizabethan clown Will Kemp in Chapelfield Gardens, Norwich – with a dash of colour added by graphic artist Gary Manders.

Anglian Annals
More moments in time
in eastern England

First published in Great Britain in paperback, September 2019
by Paul Dickson, 8 Bridge Court, Fishergate, Norwich NR3 1UE
Tel: 01603 666011   www.pauldicksonbooks.co.uk
Email: paul@pauldicksonbooks.co.uk

ISBN Paperback 9781916055032
A CIP catalogue record of this book is available from the British
Library.

Cover design by Gary Manders and Brendan Rallison
Photographs by the author, and courtesy of the Adam and Eve
pub in Norwich. Map by Andy Elsom.
Printed in Norwich by InterPrint

The Adam and Eve may be the oldest pub in Norwich – as you can see from the date on the sign, above.

Anglian annals

36 Matthew Flinders

 L'Estrange

 Smugglers

20 Cathedrals

Stamford

31 Browne

March

1 Will o' the Wisps

23 St Wendreda's

11 Prophets

Guide to the locations featured. The numbers on the map relate to chapter numbers. See Pages 11 and 12.

Cambridge

7 Days of the week

14 Guthrum

Map not to scale

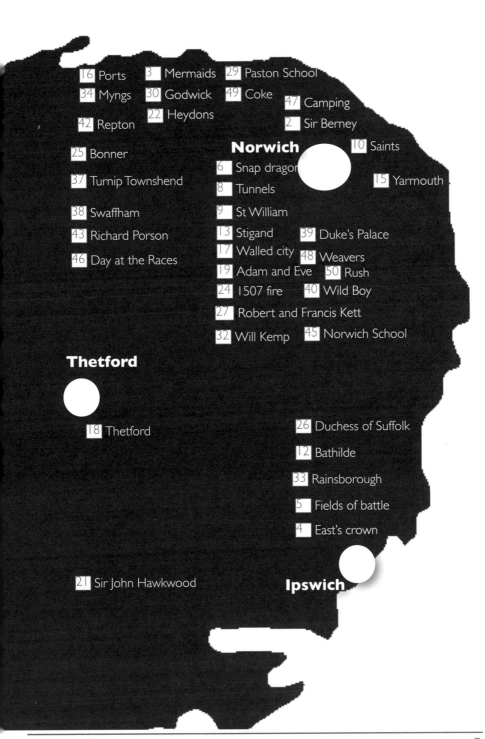

16 Ports   3 Mermaids   29 Paston School

34 Myngs   30 Godwick   49 Coke

47 Camping

22 Heydons

42 Repton

2 Sir Berney

25 Bonner

Norwich   10 Saints

37 Turnip Townshend

6 Snap dragon

8 Tunnels

15 Yarmouth

38 Swaffham

9 St William

43 Richard Porson

13 Stigand   39 Duke's Palace

46 Day at the Races

17 Walled city   48 Weavers

19 Adam and Eve   50 Rush

24 1507 fire   40 Wild Boy

27 Robert and Francis Kett

32 Will Kemp   45 Norwich School

Thetford

18 Thetford   26 Duchess of Suffolk

12 Bathilde

33 Rainsborough

5 Fields of battle

4 East's crown

21 Sir John Hawkwood   **Ipswich**

Introduction

Welcome to Anglian Annals. This is the third book in my series of short stories on the characterful and varied history of East Anglia. It follows the publications of A Moment in Time (2017) and A Place in History (2018).

Once again, you will find fifty different tales covering a wide time range, which I hope will both entertain and inform. This time I have divided the stories up into a number of distinct sections.

For the first time, I take an in-depth look at some of the colourful folklore and legends of eastern England. You'll be introduced to will o' the wisps, mermaids and mermen and Norwich's mischievous 'Snap' the Dragon. Look out also for the demonic Sir Berney Brograve, an eccentric Norfolk landowner said to have once gambled his immortal soul against Satan himself – and won.

In the section on the Middle Ages, I'll raise a glass and toast the history of my favourite pub – the Adam and Eve in Norwich, which has been serving customers since the 13th century. Readers on the side of the angels will look forward to meeting the heavenly chorus at St Wendreda's Church in Cambridgeshire, while a visit to Florence in Italy marks the resting place of an Essex boy made good, despite (or because of) his history of violence.

Coming towards the Tudor and Stuart periods, I'll ask if Bishy Barnabee – aka Bishop Edmund Bonner – deserves his reputation as a persecutor of Protestants under 'Bloody Mary', while the daring career of the Duchess of Suffolk also comes into focus. A radical Suffolk Civil War soldier turned politician, who came to a premature end, also features. On a lighter note I'll follow a Shakespearian clown – Will Kemp – on his epic nine days of dancing from London to Norwich.

The Georgian period is well represented by farming pioneer 'Turnip' Townshend, the violent and highly successful smugglers of the east coast, and a walk on the wild side into Norwich with Peter the Wild Boy. More refined readers will relish the tales of landscape gardener Humphry Repton and child genius Richard Porson.

The ancient East Anglian game of camping – a mixture of boxing and football – had its last hurrah in the 1800s, and I'll also take you for a day at the races, an era when Norfolk racehorse owners drank champagne straight from their trophies. We'll also meet notorious murderer James Rush, whose execution drew a crowd of thousands.

As with my previous two books, a number of these stories came to life in their earliest form on the pages of the Eastern Daily Press newspaper, while many are freshly researched and published here for the first time.

Once again, I am indebted to friends, family and readers for their encouragement and guidance. A big thanks to Gary Manders for his work on the cover picture of Will Kemp, Pete Kelley for his proofreading, Rita McCluskey at the Adam and Eve, as well as my publisher Paul Dickson for his continuing help and advice. Any errors are, of course, my own. The stories here are for a general rather than academic audience, but I hope you will find enough here to spark your own interest in the subject of history.

Peter Sargent
Norwich, September, 2019

Contents

Guide to pictures in colour section

i   Katherine Willoughby, Duchess of Suffolk, is buried at St James's
    Church, Spilsby.
    A carving of a mermaid in Upper Sheringham Church. The village is
    the site of a well-known mermaid legend.

ii A statue representing Tiw, the god of war, can be seen in the gardens
    at Anglesey Abbey. Tiw gives his name to our modern Tuesday.
    Blakeney St Nicholas's Church seen from the coast path. Now well
    inland, Blakeney was once a major port on the north Norfolk coast.

iii A dragon features on the top of the Ethelbert Gate to Norwich Cathedral.
    The Go-Go Dragons were a popular feature in the summer of 2015. Here,
    one is seen in Cathedral Close.
    Part of the restored rood screen at St Helen's Church, Ranworth.

iv There are many legends concerning the statues known as Samson
    and Hercules. Today these replicas stand guard outside a restaurant
    in Norwich's Tombland.
    People have been downing pints of ale at the Adam and Eve pub,
    Norwich, since at least 1249. Picture: The Adam and Eve

v   Nine days' wonder. Elizabethan funny man Will Kemp made waves
    when he danced all the way from London to Norwich.
    The Italian Job. Medieval hard man Sir John Hawkwood is honoured
    with this inscription in Florence's magnificent Duomo.
    Peter the Wild Man is remembered by this plaque at the Wild Man pub.

vi Archbishop Stigand (or Stigant) was born in Norwich, and went on
    to have a long career in the Anglo-Saxon royal court.
    The statue of Matthew Flinders and Trim the cat in Donington. A stained
    glass window in the church there recalls his exploits.

vii The Britons Arms was the only building in Elm Hill to survive the
    great fire of Norwich in 1507.
    Baconsthorpe Castle is a ruin at the end of a quiet country lane.
    Coke of Norfolk is honoured in this relief found in the grounds of Holkham
    Hall.

viii The decorated hammerbeam roof at St Wendreda's Church, March, has
    impressed visitors since the early 1500s.

Folklore and Legend

A dragon features at the Saint Ethelbert entrance to Norwich Cathedral. A reference to Old Snap, perhaps? The figure of Saint George, seen above, is depicted on the other side of the archway.

Will o' the wisps

"You are that shrewd and knavish sprite called Robin Goodfellow. Are you not he, that fright the maids of the villagery. . . mislead night-wanderers, laughing at their harm?"

If you're on the Norfolk coast at dusk, and you see a flickering blue or white light on the marshes – go no further. You may meet a lantern man.

And what would be so wrong with that?
Lantern men, will o' the wisps, will o' the wikes, jack o'lanterns, Pucks – our fertile human imagination has conjured up all sorts of colourful names for the phenomenon. It even has a fancy Latin name – ignis fatuus – or 'foolish fire'. It's hardly surprising. The sight at twilight amid marshland, bogs and swamps of an unearthly light that moves with an intelligence of its own, seems to dance and almost beckons travellers to follow its erratic course inevitably leads to all sorts of legends. And as marshes are dangerous places in the dark, following mysterious lights is never going to end well.

The light fantastic. . .
Tales of lantern men are not unique to East Anglia. They go under a variety of names throughout Britain, Europe and North America. Shakespeare's mischievous Puck in A Midsummer Night's Dream is one of these supernatural characters, and the subject of the quotation at the top of this chapter. They share certain characteristics; otherworldly creatures who deliberately shine lights to attract the curious, then lead them into danger, even death by drowning in thick mud or water. Because the lights seemed to flicker and bob around, the story went that the fairy folk were dancing. Fairies in history were not the harmless, fluffy little things we think of now, but an underworld spirit to treat warily. In East Anglian folklore they were often the spirits of

people who met a violent death, or lived an evil life. Heard's Holde at Irstead was said to be the haunt of a man named Heard who died there. His restless spirit could enter neither Heaven nor Hell, and was said to haunt the marsh. Countrymen said the best thing to do on meeting a lantern man was to throw yourself flat on your face and hold your breath until the spirit had passed by, for it was believed they could steal your breath from your body. What's more, you should never shine a light yourself, as that would attract them.

Dangerous characters. . .
Above all, the advice was never to mock them. Puck, or Robin Goodfellow as he was known in Elizabethan times, could be a good friend, but a terrible enemy. Shakespeare would have known all about him and his master, Oberon 'King of the Fairies'. Legend had it that if you left out food and drink for Puck, he'd do you a good turn, even do your housework. But if you crossed him and his kind, you'd find buckets knocked over, milk stolen, your beer spoiled. Openly scorn the lantern men, and they might chase you home and burn down your house. It could be worse; you could be led to your death. According to a 200-year-old legend a wherryman named Joseph Bexfield fell into this trap. Joseph plied the River Yare between Norwich and Yarmouth, transporting goods along this important trade highway. One night he and his crew moored up at Thurlton Staithe, and walked along a track through the marshes to the White Horse inn. From the warmth and comfort of the inn, the men could see lights in the marsh. Joseph laughed when warned not to go out, instead venturing back to the boat along the path. He was never seen alive again; three days later his body was found in the Yare near Reedham. Aged 38, Joseph left a wife and children, and is said to haunt the area. Or perhaps he just fell in the river in the dark. . . His gravestone at All Saints' Church, Thurlton, merely records he was drowned in August, 1809. But this tale added to a body of folklore that stretched along the coast. At one time Cromer was said to be a haunt of lantern men, while at Sheringham it was the spirits of drowned sailors, called 'yow-yows', who lured the unwary. In

the fens of Norfolk, Lincolnshire and Cambridgeshire, the marshes were known to be dangerous. There the spirits were called 'will o' the wikes', and lurked in the as yet undrained wetland. Puck also loomed large in the imagination; in the fenland town of March, Cambridgeshire, there is a Robin Goodfellows Lane to this day. It seemed most people treated the spirits with respect. During the Reformation, the Church denounced these beliefs as superstitious idolatry, and described the spirits as 'devils'. Despite this, in country areas these beliefs lived on for centuries. In different parts of the country they had other names – in Shropshire they are 'Will the Smith, in Lancashire 'Peg-a-Lantern'.

And the sensible, rational explanation?
It's now generally believed will o' the wisps are a natural phenomenon. Organic decay of marsh vegetation leads to the oxidisation of phosphine and methane, which results in spontaneous ignition. When the marshes were drained, the lights largely disappeared; in any case, modern light pollution would probably make the lights hard to see. But does the scientific theory explain the flickering movements? Another idea is that barn owls have luminescent plumage that can reflect light from the moon and appear as will o' the wisps.

So, what should I do if see a light on the marsh at night?
Don't panic! Probably stay in the pub. Perhaps our ancestors had a point – show a little respect and make a friend, not an enemy, of Puck, and all will be well.

"So good night to you all.
Give me your hands, if we be friends
And Robin shall restore amends".
(Puck's final words in A Midsummer Night's Dream).

Owd Sir Berney

He counted among his friends and opponents the Devil, smugglers, pugnacious chimney sweeps and ghostly knights. He was one of the most notorious and colourful gentlemen of 18th century Norfolk. Meet 'Owd Sir Berney' Brograve.

Sounds like another made-up character

Sir Berney Brograve, 1st Baronet, was as real as any other man - only a little more so. A scion of a wild family, the stories about him got taller as time went on, but he must have been quite a character. More than 200 years since his death they have not forgotten Sir Berney in north Norfolk. The family was originally from Essex. In 1733 his father Thomas bought the Norfolk manors of Worstead, Waxham and Horsey. Although Worstead was a famous weaving centre, coastal Waxham and Horsey were remote, marshy areas, sparsely populated and regarded as the haunt of marsh spirits and witches. Which suited Thomas Brograve rather well, as he moved his family into Waxham Hall. He got a reputation as a boisterous gentleman and a duellist. The story goes that in 1728 he fought a duel in Hyde Park, London, with a Norfolk man named Henry Branthwayt. After the two had fired pistols at one another, and missed, they drew swords. Brograve ran his man through the left breast, and he died immediately. "Having kissed the dead body, he waved his hat for the coach. . . and made off." Duelling was strictly illegal, though the courts often winked at it. Nevertheless it was prudent not to hang around.

Like father, like son

Berney Brograve – apparently he was named Julian after his mother, Julia, but was known locally as Berney – was a brawler, a fighter and a terror to his neighbours. He was also an improving landlord keen to maximise the income from his sprawling, but hitherto unproductive, lands. The family had two main properties; Waxham Hall had been built by the Woodville family in the 16th century, while Sir Berney had architect James Wyatt design him a house at Worstead, "a fine red-brick mansion, situated with a noble park of 400 acres with a lake covering eight and a quarter acres". To drain his marshy land Brograve built a windpump on what became known as the Brograve Level. It drained excess water into the new man-made navigation, the Waxham New Cut. In 1791, aged 65, he was made a baronet.

So far, so normal. . .

Brograve was eccentric. He cut an old-fashioned figure even for the mid-18th century. Described as 'of slovenly appearance' and 'Bacchanalian', he was usually under the influence of drink. At his farm he had 100 men working, all apparently lodged at Worstead, dining together in the great hall. To complete this medieval picture of a country squire, Sir Berney was said to be the last man in Norfolk to keep his own jester. Rumour had it he was in cahoots with local smugglers; in 1780, passing smuggling vessels fired a cannon salute to him at his coastal home at Waxham. Quick to anger, he was said to be happiest in a punch-up. Once he challenged a chimney sweep to a fight, offering to pay him double if he bested him or nothing if he lost. Needless to say, Brograve came up trumps. His reputation spread to the supernatural; tradition had it that each New Year's Eve he was joined by the ghosts of various ancestral knights killed violently or in battle, who dined with him until morning, then vanished for another 12 months.

Sounds vaguely devilish

Sir Berney knew the Devil, who seemed to be no stranger to Norfolk. Two local legends stand out, both attesting to his alleged bravado and shamelessness. At Worstead he wagered his immortal soul to Satan, bragging he could mow a field of beans quicker than the Devil. Although he soon thought better of it, and tried to back out of the bet, the Devil demanded his due. Sir Berney decided to cheat. He asked a blacksmith to make small iron rods up to the height of the beanstalks that the Devil had to cut. Sure enough, as the two protagonists began to cut rows of stalks with their scythes, the Devil blunted his blade on the iron. Sir Berney drew ahead, and the Devil gave up, with ill grace. Having got away with that, in a later tale he actually sold his soul. Sure enough, when he died, he gave himself up to the Devil, but Satan, wary of the old rogue's reputation, wouldn't have him. Sir Berney asked him where he should go, getting the reply: "Go to hell!" – on which he stayed, and the Devil was stuck with him.

A loveable rogue?

In reality the Brograves were prominent Norfolk gentry. Berney married heiresses twice, producing a total of 15 children, many of whom died in infancy, as, sadly, was all too common then. The baronet died in 1797, and was succeeded by his son, George. He maintained the family's reputation, keeping a pack of hounds who terrified the neighbourhood. On the other hand, he was a lieutenant-colonel of the Norfolk Militia and a High Sheriff of Norfolk in 1802 – so he can't have been all bad. There is no doubt these tall tales grew with the telling. His life was soured by a notorious divorce case, after his wife absconded with her lover. Although the court took the husband's side, as was usual 200 years ago, his reputation was damaged. He died intestate in 1828, and the family title perished with him. A younger brother, Roger, was a compulsive gambler. In 1813 he lost the enormous sum of £10,000 at Newmarket racecourse. "Unable to answer his engagements," ie pay his debts, he shot himself with a duelling pistol in bed. A jury brought in a verdict of insanity. The family name lives on in the Brograve Level, while the mill was last worked in 1930. One mile north of Horsey Mere, it is a Grade Two listed building, but derelict and unsafe to enter. Worstead House was demolished in 1937.

And Owd Sir Berney?

Never one for a quiet exit, it is said that on dark, stormy nights around Waxham and Worstead he still rides out on his horse. One step ahead of the Devil, no doubt, who is still after his soul.

Mermaids ahoy!

In Upper Sheringham church you will find a mysterious carving. It depicts a mermaid, and reflects one of the most alluring myths that has haunted men's minds for centuries.

Another fishy tale. . .

Mermaids, as we understand them, are mythical creatures from the sea with a woman's head and torso and a fish's tail. The word comes from the Old English for the sea – mere – and maid is the old-fashioned term for a young woman. Their male equivalent is the merman, but, as we shall see, they have not captured the imagination of sailors quite so vividly. Long hours and days spent gazing out at sea can play havoc with a man's imagination. But it was not just seafaring men who were enchanted by the idea of mermaids – the legend spread far inland and across the world. At All Saints Church, Upper Sheringham, the story goes that some time during the 15th century a service was taking place. As the beadle (a church official) looked to the door he saw a young girl open it up and peek into the church. To his surprise he saw she had a fish's tail. The beadle shooed her away, slamming the door in her face for everyone knew that mermaids had no soul and were not allowed in God's house. Undeterred, the mermaid sneaked back in again while the beadle's back was turned, and sat in the pew to listen to the service. Other versions of the tale insist the mermaid had been washed up on Sheringham beach in rough weather, and hauled herself (or should that be slithered?) up the hill to the church in search of a soul. And that is why a mermaid is carved into a pew end, and the village sign has an illustration of a pair of mermaids around the name.

Nice story. . . totally made up, surely!

One theory is that mermaids were at one time a symbol of prostitution. These supposed sexual predators of the sea became a metaphor for loose women. It could be that the origins of the Upper Sheringham tale concern a notorious prostitute who scandalised parishioners, and the story had grown with the telling. If so it is just another thread to a fantasy that has been going on since ancient times. To the ancient Assyrians in 1000BC the origins of the legend go back to a goddess, Atargatis – who fell in love with a mortal, but turned herself into an aquatic creature in grief after inadvertently causing his death. To the Ancient Greeks they were the Sirens, alluring creatures who sat on the rocks and sang to sailors, distracting them and causing them to founder in dangerous shallow waters – although the Sirens were sometimes seen as birdlike characters rather than humanoid. They also feature in the tales of the Arabian Nights, as 'Sea People'.

Good. . . or bad?

On the whole, bad. In British folklore the sighting of a mermaid either predicts disaster or causes it. They are also a sign of bad weather to come. Not only are they seen at sea, but in rivers and freshwater lakes. The Lorelei of the German Rhine, as depicted by the likes of Richard Wagner, are a case in point. These tales are not just European in origin, spreading to such places as Japan and the Philippines. Old tales tell of mermaids dragging sailors into the depths and crushing the life out of them. More benign mermaids are said to just forget that humans cannot breathe underwater, so their attempts to revive drowning sailors usually end in disaster. For churchmen, such as the Upper Sheringham beadle, the worst aspect of mermaids was they had no souls, so had to be wicked. Although merfolk were said to live for up to 300 years, they simply disappeared into nothing when they eventually died. Others were less fussy. Our rather more positive view of mermaids is probably influenced by Hans Christian Andersen. His Little Mermaid, written in 1837, was a rather more innocent creation. She was willing to give up her life in the sea in exchange for an eternal soul and the love of a human prince. Eventually, despite being thwarted in her desire to marry a prince, she won her soul by doing good deeds. It's a long way from dragging sailors to a watery grave! The Danes, as enchanted by the myth as any seafarer, built a bronze statue of a mermaid in Copenhagen harbour in honour of their great storyteller.

What about mermen?

They don't really get a look in. Supposedly rather ugly, they have simply failed to captured the imagination. One story is probably based on fact. At Orford in Suffolk, a tale persists of a merman who was captured in a fisherman's net in 1207. Naked and "covered in hair with a long shaggy beard", when taken into a church "he showed no signs of reverence or belief," wrote a contemporary chronicler, Ralph of Coggleshall. He would eat anything given him, and was particularly keen on raw fish. The creature was imprisoned in the castle. There, the garrison mistreated him. He "would not talk, although oft times hung up by his feet and harshly tortured". Probably tiring of such terrible torments, he eventually escaped back to sea, never to be seen again.

And mermaids today?

Divested of their dark origins, mermaids have been given the full Disney and Hollywood treatment in modern times, usually pictured as young and beautiful women with no sinister implications. A number of pubs and inns bear the name, such as the Mermaid Inn at Elsing, Dereham, Hedenham, near Bungay, and – far inland – Huntingdon, Cambridgeshire. Look out also for The Mermaid's Slipper at Stalham. Elsewhere in our region, the Mermaid at Surfleet in Lincolnshire stands by the River Glen. (By the by, the name came in 223rd on a recent list of British pub names listed by website pubsgalore.co.uk, with 21 in all. The Red Lion is by far the most popular name, with 567 across the country.)

Anything else?

Local rockpoolers come across mermaid's purses. These are egg capsules left by some sharks, skates and dogfish which resemble a sort of pouch. Presumably, they are not filled with some sort of mermaid currency. . .

The crown of the east

Late in the 19th century East Anglia acquired its own distinctive flag. At its heart was the image of three crowns, reflecting a persistent legend of a time when this region formed an independent kingdom.

What's the significance?

The great ghost story writer M R (Montague Rhodes) James gave the tale its most famous outing. In his classic story A Warning to the Curious, he outlines the legend of the three crowns of East Anglia. Dating from the early years of an independent kingdom in these parts – some 1,500 years ago – it adds a mystical touch to the history of a time when this region was the dominant force in England. East Anglia traces its origins to the warrior elite who came here from northern Germany in the fourth and fifth centuries from an area known as Angeln – the Angles. Historians are divided as to how many Angles came here; were they a small but influential number, an elite warrior caste who subsequently dominated the region, or was the Angles' supremacy the result of mass migration? At all events, by the sixth century this region, modern Norfolk, Suffolk and parts of Cambridgeshire, had a common identity as Angles – or English. In the 520s the North-folk and South-folk merged, forging a powerful kingdom. A century later this kingdom briefly became the prominent force in the divided island. Under its King Raedwald, it defeated other powers, such as Northumbria, to lord it over its neighbours for a few years. Raedwald himself was given a magnificent burial in the 620s; it is believed he was the king buried in a longship along with priceless treasures which was excavated at Sutton Hoo, near Woodbridge, Suffolk, in 1939. Here was a king powerful and rich enough to afford three crowns.

It couldn't last. . .

Decline set in quickly. The Mercian kingdom to the west (think of it as the modern midlands) coveted its eastern neighbour's land. King Offa – the man who built the famous 'dyke' fortification to hem in the Welsh – invited the young East Anglian king Ethelbert to marry his daughter. Once his future son-in-law travelled to Hereford, he was unceremoniously murdered and Offa took control of his kingdom. An East Anglian revolt in 825 restored independence. In the 860s another young king was invited from his home in Germany to rule in the east. His name was Edmund, and his reign was rudely interrupted by another band of invaders. The Viking Danes defeated and killed Edmund in Suffolk in 869, after which he was made a saint. His shrine at Bury St Edmunds became a wealthy abbey popular with pilgrims. The Vikings, under Guthrum the Dane, ruled in East Anglia for the next few decades. English armies commanded by the kings of Wessex subsequently wrested the area back in a series of campaigns along the turbulent frontier, but East Anglian independence was dead for ever as it eventually joined a united England.

Was it really the end of independence?

We've always had a 'do different' approach here. In its quiet, stubborn and understated way, East Anglia never quite forgot its history. Which is probably why the legend of the three crowns was born. Three crowns is a heraldic device used by Swedish royalty to this day – and it is from Sweden that the Wuffing royal dynasty – to which the East Anglian kings belonged – first emigrated to England. The legend goes that three of King Edmund's ninth century crowns were buried on the shore – one of them most likely at Aldeburgh in Suffolk – to ward off subsequent invasions. As mentioned above, M R James took up the story. This distinguished Cambridge medieval scholar knew his history and folklore, and drew on it for many of his chilling tales, written early in the 20th century. A Warning to the Curious is set in the fictional Seaburgh, which is based on Aldeburgh. A young scholar named Paxton is drawn to the legend like a moth to the flame, and discovers from a churchwarden that the three crowns were buried along the coast at different places after Edmund's death. They were meant to ward off invaders – "the Danes, French or Germans". One crown was dug up at Rendlesham, near the coast, in 1687 and melted down for its precious metal, another was washed away by coastal erosion (could this be at Dunwich, the once thriving port in medieval times, now long since submerged underneath the sea?) while the other was still there. In the story, the crown is guarded by members of the local Ager family, the last of whom has recently died. Paxton discovers the crown on the beach, digs it up – but from then on is never quite alone. It seems he has upset the implacable guardians of the last crown, from beyond the grave. He attempts to return the crown to its hiding place, but the damage has already been done. Needless to say, it all ends rather badly for the greedy archaeologist.

Any truth in this legend?
No Anglo-Saxon crown has ever been found. The kings of the old English didn't really go in for them. At the Sutton Hoo ship burial site, all sorts of treasures have been discovered; swords, shields, helmets and other symbolic devices, but no crown. A number of modern writers and treasure hunters have been inspired by M R James's story, but, like King John's lost treasure in The Wash, it seems unlikely anything will ever be found. Besides, who wants to upset the guardians of the crowns?

And these days?
Very few people have any belief in this legend now. It was not always so. In 1900 one George Henry Langham devised an East Anglian flag. It displayed the coat of arms of the Wuffings – King Raedwald's Scandinavian dynasty; three crowns on a blue shield, the colour of the Swedish flag. This image was superimposed on a Cross of Saint George, which is of course the modern symbol of England – always popular when the national football team does well at World Cups! On a local note, Bury St Edmunds' heraldic shield has three crowns and two arrows through each crown, representing the martyred King Edmund, who was said to have been executed by Viking archers.

Fields of battle

East Anglia has escaped the worst of the battles that once scarred the British Isles. Its geographical position meant it avoided border raids and the worst of the civil wars. But it hasn't been all peace and quiet. There has been fighting here – the hard part is working out fact from fiction.

A history of violence?

Legend surrounds sites in the region where, it is claimed, battles were fought between Romans and Britons, Vikings and Anglo-Saxons, French and English – and Oliver Cromwell against just about anyone who fancied a go. Often they are based on reality – as at Blythburgh for example – but others are based on a gruesome name – such as Bloodgate at South Creake, or stories handed down by word of mouth until they are enshrined in folklore.

Start with the facts

The earliest recorded battle in East Anglia came in the fenland. At Stonea, near March in Cambridgeshire, Roman forces overcame British defenders (probably a branch of the Iceni tribe) in about 47AD. The site of this battle remains open to dispute, with other historians feeling it more likely to have happened in Norfolk, the heartland of the Iceni; at Thetford an Iceni palace has been excavated, and it may have been the main settlement of Boudica's people. The decisive battles of her rising against Rome in 61AD came around Colchester, St Albans and London, but this has not stopped legends of clashes between Roman and Briton in Norfolk. At Bergh Apton a tradition persists of a battle fought nearby. Feltwell also claims a slice of the Boudica story, with tales of a scrap against the Romans, while at Garboldisham, excavated Bronze Age earthworks known as the Devil's Ditch were once thought to hold the Iceni queen's grave.

Any truth in these tales?

Often the key is in the name. 'Bergh', or 'Burgh' implies a Saxon word for a fortress – our modern 'borough' comes from this. So Bergh Apton may have been a fort, while Burgh St Peter could be another defensive place – hence legends of a battle fought there between two unidentified forces. The word 'battle' may just refer to some random act of violence, rather than a pitched fight between armies. Perhaps the name of a place was the spur for the stories. Bloodgate Hill at South Creake was the site of an Iron Age fort (pre-dating Boudica by several centuries). The name sounds gruesome, but on 17th century maps the area was called Burgh Dykes, implying people knew it had been a fortress – perhaps 'Bloodgate' came later. Similarly, Bloodslade at Bacton is said to have been a battleground. Blood Hills at West Somerton not only has a Viking battle legend, but a Gibbet Hill besides. We can be fairly sure, however, that Blythburgh was the site of a major event. In 653/4 East Anglia's king Aenna and his son were killed by invading Mercians from the midlands. The actual site of the battle is vague, being referred to as Bulcamp, but historians believe it was fought a mile away from Blythburgh. The king was buried there, at the site of today's church.

What about the Vikings?

The Danes invaded East Anglia in 869 and conquered it rapidly. They defeated and killed King Edmund, who subsequently became a saint. But where were the battles fought? History gets vague, so legend takes over. Some say Edmund lost at Thetford, following a siege. There's logic here; Thetford was an Anglo-Saxon bastion, and the likeliest spot for the king's execution was at nearby Hoxne. Other places lay claim to Edmund's last stand. At Attleborough Bunn's Bank earthwork may have been built to withstand the Danes; Drayton's Blood Dale, by the River Wensum, is another site with claims to an English vs Vikings clash; while the feature known as The Great Stone of Lyng is said to be where Edmund fought the Danes, then retreated to Castle Acre (actually, the stone's a glacial boulder – but that spoils a good story). At Rushford, graves are said to be those of Edmund's warriors, and at Tutt

Hill a shepherd is supposed to have shown the Danes a way into Thetford Castle. This last really does sound like a legend, repeating tales spun by ancient Greeks about traitors showing Persians a secret route through the pass at Thermopylae, resulting in the fight to the death by the 300 Spartans. Two more incidents came in the early 11th century. In 1004 Swein Forkbeard attacked Norwich and Thetford. The English, under Ealdorman (Earl) Ulfcytel, caught up with them at Wretham Heath and fought the Danes to a bloody standstill, after which the invaders retreated. In the words of the Anglo-Saxon Chronicle: "As they themselves said they never met with harder battle skill among the English than Ulfcytel brought to them." Six years later Swein's Danes won another battle at Ringmere, south of Thetford.

In 903 the English fought a vital battle in the fens against the Danes. Following the death of Alfred the Great his son Edward became king. His cousin, the Atheling (king's son) Aethelwold, whose father had been Alfred's elder brother and king before him, said he had the better right to the crown of Wessex. To further his claim he joined forces with the Northumbrian and East Anglian Vikings.

These unlikely allies broke the uneasy truce between the sides. The Norse fleet assembled and raided in Mercia and North Wessex. Edward retaliated by counter-attacking in the east. In mid-December the two sides fought a pitched battle, the site of which is today identified as Holme, Cambridgeshire. (It's just off the A1, east of Sawtry.) It was a messy, bloody fight with heavy casualties on both sides. According to the Anglo-Saxon Chronicle, the Danes lost "Eohric their king, atheling Aethelwold, who had lured them into peace-breaking. . . and very many besides". On the English side, there was some confusion about the role of the Kentish contingent, who appear to have disobeyed orders. They "stayed on there against the king's command and seven messages he had sent to them". Kentish ealdormen Sigulf and Sigelm were killed. "Of the Danes there were more killed, though they had the battlefield." The Danes may have won, but their heavy losses made it a pyrrhic victory. Alfred's successors were well on their way to uniting England as one nation.

Some peace and quiet please!

East Anglia was fortunate to escape the worst bloodshed and devastation of the Norman Conquest, although guerrilla leader Hereward the Wake turned the Isle of Ely into his fenland bastion. The Normans made Norwich their power base in the east. During the medieval period there were a number of attempted seaborne invasions; in 1173 the people of Dunwich, then an important port, turned back rebels opposing King Henry II. In 1381 Norfolk rebels joined the Peasants' Revolt. They seized Norwich and attacked Great Yarmouth before being defeated by royal forces led by the Bishop of Norwich. They made their last stand near North Walsham. Two centuries later Robert Kett's peasant rebels came a cropper just outside Norwich when they took on an army of government mercenaries.

Any civil war scraps?

Lucky East Anglia also missed the carnage of the civil wars of the 1640s. The only real unpleasantness came when Lynn rose for the king in 1643. Oliver Cromwell besieged the town, handing over to Parliamentary forces under the Earl of Manchester, who forced the Royalists to surrender. Cromwell crops up in many legends; at Bacton, for example, he is said to have bombarded the former monastery of Bromholm. One place where he was actually documented as being involved in a siege was Crowland in the Lincolnshire fens. In the spring of 1643, early in the civil war, the town's Royalists kidnapped the Puritan minister of nearby Spalding along with other citizens. Parliamentary forces besieged the town, with its iconic ruined abbey, aided by Oliver Cromwell's contingent. Eventually, Crowland fell. Cromwell moved on to greater things. Perhaps Oliver has been mixed up in legends associated with another famous Cromwell – his distant kinsman Thomas, Henry VIII's right hand man, who dissolved the monasteries in the 1530s. That's the nature of legends; any kind of upheaval tends to be attributed to the most famous people of the day – so Boudica, King Edmund and the Cromwells will forever be associated with East Anglian battlefields.

Snap the dragon

'Snap, Snap, steal a boy's cap; give him a penny, he'll give it back."
This rhyme, popular on the streets of Norwich in the late 19th century, is part of a popular piece of the city's folklore – one that goes back several centuries.

Sounds like a mischievous character

The snapdragon, known as 'Old Snap', has terrified and delighted Norwich city people since the Middle Ages. Once part of a religious rite, he became a symbol of corporate pageantry, then an excuse for riotous behaviour before being rehabilitated today in the annual July Lord Mayor's Procession. As we will see, Snap is not the only dragon to prowl the streets of Norwich.

Some sort of panto character?

In the Norwich Castle Museum is a painted canvas dragon, made over a wooden frame. Like a panto, or hobby horse, it is meant to be carried by a man within the framework. The one in the museum is said to date from 1795, but the first Snap was probably made in the early 1400s. It was in 1349 that King Edward III chose Saint George as England's patron saint. Supposedly a Roman soldier of Middle Eastern origin martyred in the early fourth century AD, George became popular during the Crusades with chivalrous knights. His cult spread to many countries, and today he is patron saint of Russia, Greece, Catalonia, Ethiopia, Georgia, Lithuania, the island of Gozo, near Malta, and Portugal, as well as England. On April 23 each year, for example, in tiny Gozo church bells ring out and flags with the red cross are waved in honour of the saint. Closer to home, a number of guilds were dedicated to Saint George. These were trade associations with religious, charitable and sociable characteristics. Norwich's Guild and Fraternity of Saint George was founded in 1389, and there were others elsewhere; for example, Lynn's was founded in 1376.

What did they do?

Guilds had been around for centuries. They collected money for the poor and members who fell into need, especially their families if breadwinners died or became too ill to work. But they were also important in religious terms. The Norwich guild had a chapel at the cathedral, and paid a priest to say Mass for members each day. On Saint George's feast day, a procession and service was held, and a play enacted. A member dressed as the saint, who had to rescue a maiden – Saint Margaret – from the dragon. Old Snap entered Norwich folklore, his first recorded archive entry being in 1408. With his snapping jaws, he would caper among the crowd, a complex figure of both fun and fear. Writing as late as the 18th century, local historian Benjamin Mackerell said: "The Dragon, carried by a Man in the body of it, gave great diversion to the common People. They always seemed to fear it when it was near them, but always looked upon it with pleasure when it was a distance from them." Snap was accompanied by the Whifflers, who wore distinctive scarlet satin breeches, white satin jerkins and hats with feathers and ribbons, and carried drawn swords. The comical 'dick fools' wore red and yellow caps with fox tails and small bells. Also in the procession were the city Waits (musicians), cathedral choristers and city officials. An inscription in Norwich Castle's grounds records some possible dialogue spoken by Saint George as he tackled Snap: "Should twenty thousand dragons rise, I'd fight them all before your eyes! And now I'll slay the dragon, my wonders to begin. A fell and fiery dragon he, but I will clip his wing."

All good fun

The Guild became powerful in Norwich after it was given a Royal Charter by King Henry V in 1417. Soon it dominated local government, and the Saint George's Day feast and procession became combined with the Mayor-making ceremony. At its height, up to 800 people would eat at the Guildhall. Everything changed at the Reformation. In 1548, the Protestant government of Edward VI abolished Guilds as "superstitious". The Norwich Guild changed its name to "The

Company and Citizens of Saint George". Saints George and Margaret were written out of the tale, but Snap the Dragon survived, "for pastime, the Dragon to come and shew himself as in other years". He was just too popular to get rid of. So it went on; the Company dominated local politics and the pageantry continued. But in 1729 Alderman William Clark attacked its legality and it collapsed within two years, surrendering its assets to the local corporation. Legislation in 1835 – the Municipal Corporations Act – abolished many long-held traditions, such as the pageantry surrounding Mayor-making, as part of a crackdown on corruption. The dragon lived on, stripped of his corporate identity. Groups such as the Pockthorpe Guild, formed in 1772, made their own Snap. Going from pub to pub, it became a way of raising funds. There was also a dragon paraded at Costessey during mayor-making week. During the 19th century, Snap and his attendants became associated with disorderly behaviour, such as stealing boys' caps, as the rhyme at the head of this story suggests. The orderly society of the early 20th century put a stop to it. A well-behaved Snap has been rehabilitated, and is paraded each July through the city. He is still accompanied by the Whifflers, who carry drawn swords, like their predecessors.

A city for dragons

Norwich has a penchant for dragons. Tales involving these fire-eaters date back to pre-Christian times, as does the legend of Saint George, which has similarities with the ancient Greek Perseus and Andromeda, and dragons feature in Arthurian mythology. There is a dragon motif in the merchant's hall in King Street, now known as Dragon Hall. A dragon and Saint George are carved on Saint Ethelbert's Gate at the entrance to the cathedral. Snap also appears on the CAMRA Norwich Beer Festival logo each October. He is the symbol of the city. In 2009 Norwich held its first Festival of Dragons to commemorate their presence. Saint George remained popular in the plays of 'mummers', who carried on until the late 19th century. A good description of their antics can be found in Thomas Hardy's Return of the Native.

Just another day

**In the grounds of Anglesey Abbey, near Cambridge, stands a statue
of an Anglo-Saxon god called Tiw. He gives his name to our
Tuesday – but why? And why are there seven days in a week?**

There have always been seven days in a week, haven't there?
We can't be sure people here in Britain, or elsewhere, have always
numbered their weeks thus. Only when society became organised, and
a priestly caste emerged to explain the mysteries of the heavens, did
we need to give a name to each day. Ever since the ancient Greeks
started looking at the stars, dividing our time into sevens has been the
norm. It was the group of philosophers known as the Stoics who
devised the names of the planets according to their relationship with
the Earth; Saturn, Jupiter, Mars, Sun, Venus, Mercury, Moon. Their
system, the Ptolemaic, was based on the notion that these heavenly
bodies presided over the hours of our days. It was only natural to
regard them as divine beings, and name our days of the week after
them. Between the first and third centuries AD the Roman Empire
established the seven-day week, and it spread from there. In Britain,
other influences came to the fore. Despite 400 years of Roman rule,
only one of our days retains its Roman name. The others reflect
Germanic and Scandinavian legends, though even these are influenced
by Roman gods and goddesses. This has a fancy Latin name,
interpretatio romanā; the characteristics of a Roman deity are transferred
to a local god.

Sunday

This comes from the Roman *dies solis*, day of the sun, and reflects the
growing cult of sun worship under the Empire. The Roman festival of
sol invictus, the Unconquered Sun, celebrated the rebirth of the sun
following the winter solstice. As it fell on December 25, some have seen
it as a precursor to Christmas. But, while 'Romance' languages such as

French, Italian and Spanish have changed the day's name to 'lord's day' (eg Dimanche or Domingo) to honour its Christian connotations, here in the north its pagan name remains. Our close neighbours the Germans (Sonntag) and Dutch (Zontag) retain the Sun's prominence in this first day of the week.

Monday
In keeping with the astrological theme, this is the 'moon's day'. To the Romans it was sacred to the moon goddess, and this is reflected in the French 'lundi' after the Latin word for the moon goddess, 'Luna'. For the Germans, it is Montag and the Dutch call it Maandag.

Tuesday
So far we have kept in line with the rest of Europe. But Tiw (Tyr to the Scandinavians) seems to break the mould. Tiw was a pretty belligerent fellow, being keen on single combat and warfare. According to Norse legend, he was renowned for his courage. When the other gods were at a loss to know what to do with the savage wolf Fenrir, Tiw placed his hand in the wolf's mouth in a bid to bind him. Although he lost his hand, he succeeded, and Fenrir is, according to legend, bound until the day the world ends. Here's a link with the Romans. They knew this day as that of Mars, their god of war (mardi in French). Perhaps the early English wanted to honour the day devoted to the god of war with one of their own. The Germans, oddly enough, call their Tuesday Dienstag, assembly day. Well, it's up to them, isn't it?

Wednesday
This is Wodin's day – or Odin's day. Wodin was an Old English god and Odin was the chief of the Norse gods; the two seem to have merged. Not much connection, it would seem, with the Romans' Mercury, whose day this is. Wasn't he just the messenger of the gods? The link is that Wodin/Odin carried the dead off the field of battle, a merciful role that Mercury fulfilled for the Romans. The French, true to their Latin roots, call this Mercredi, while the Germans, with admirable

literal-mindedness, reckon it's Mittwoch – midweek. Early Anglo-Saxon kings claimed descent from Wodin, so in theory our present Queen is related to him.

Thursday

This is Thor's Day. Thor is one of the best known of the Norse gods, renowned for his hammer, and said to be able to conjure up thunder, lightning and storms. His hammer emblem became a show of pagan defiance in Scandinavia as Christianity advanced. Perhaps it's surprising the early Church didn't try to change the name once they had converted the English – perhaps it was too ingrained by then. Before its meaning was perverted by the Nazis, the Swastika symbol denoted Thor's lightning. 'Donner' means 'thunder' in German, so their 'Donnerstag' literally means 'Thunder-day'. The Romans? This was their day sacred to Jupiter, or Jove, king of the gods, so they dubbed it *dies Jovis*. The French have followed suit, calling it jeudi.

Friday

Freya was the Germanic and Norse goddess of fertility, love and beauty, sometimes known as Frigg. The Roman Venus did the same job for them, so here's another example of a locally sourced goddess quite rightly displacing a foreign imperial one. Freya was a versatile lady, riding in a chariot driven by two (presumably large) cats. She is said to have received half of those slain in battle; the rest go to Valhalla. The Romans named Friday *dies veneris*, the French vendredi and the Germans are with us again, with Freitag.

Saturday

Finally, the day that has stayed Roman. Their Saturn's Day (*dies saturni*) became the Anglo-Saxon sater daeg, the French samedi and the German Samstag. Saturn was the Roman god of agriculture, the harvest and civilization and government (which follow on from agriculture). He was also the father of Jupiter, and is depicted carrying a sickle in his left hand and a bundle of wheat in his right.

Tunnels and treasure

There's more to East Anglia than we see on the surface, if we were to believe all the legends.

Second only to ghost stories are the many yarns containing secret tunnels. They usually involve old abbeys and churches, there's an element of skulduggery – and a varied cast including everything from sword-wielding Celtic kings to lost pigs. The truth is rather more prosaic than the colourful myths that have been spun for generations. Sadly, most of the tunnels uncovered over the centuries turned out to be little more than drainage conduits. But that hasn't stopped people from telling the stories. And maybe there's a germ of truth in there, if we dig deep enough. Take Bromholm Priory. There's little left to see of this once thriving religious site, near Bacton on the Norfolk coast. In its pomp it was a place of pilgrimage. After a crusading soldier returned from the East in the 1200s with a piece of the 'True Cross' used at Christ's crucifixion, the rich and powerful flocked to see it. This probably led to rumours that there is still buried treasure at the site, particularly as there was no sign of the relic at the Dissolution of the 1530s. The tale persists that a tunnel runs from the priory to Gimingham Hall, four miles away. Midway between the two, it is said to be divided by a pair of golden gates. Similarly, there is supposed to be a tunnel from Beeston Priory to a wayside cross at Gresham, and from there to the remains of Gresham Castle. The image of a golden calf is hidden, though no-one has yet found either tunnel or calf. Nor is there any evidence of another tunnel, from St Benet's Abbey in the Broads to nearby St Helen's Church, Ranworth, also said to be the repository of treasure.

Hmmm. . . that's hardly surprising

There's better, albeit anecdotal evidence of tunnels from Binham Priory to the shrine at Walsingham, and to the port of Blakeney, supposedly emerging at its 14th century guildhall. This has given rise to the tale of the fiddler, Jimmy Griggs, and his dog, Tap. Followed by a large crowd, the fiddler entered the tunnel, vowing to discover what was inside. He never re-emerged. A similar tale is told of another fiddler, lost forever in the Blakeney tunnel, this time accompanied by a cat. Other legends speak of tunnels from St Faith's Priory, Horsham, to the castle at Horsford. Ingham Priory had a tunnel leading to the nearby manor house. When dug up in the 19th century it was found to contain a number of skeletons, but the tunnel was never explored and was sealed up again. Similarly, there is said to be a tunnel between Old Buckenham priory and neighbouring New Buckenham castle. Hickling Priory tops the lot. It not only has a tunnel leading to the marshes, but a resident mad monk to haunt it.

Any reason to build these tunnels?

A consistent theme is the link between monasteries and pubs. For example, Greyfriars in King's Lynn is meant to have a tunnel to the White Hart inn, while chroniclers mentioned a passage from Norwich Cathedral to a nearby pub. While the image of thirsty monks digging their way out for a sneaky pint is a tempting one, it seems that the Lynn tunnel actually led to a well for fresh water. Another tunnel legend involves a former queen of England. Isabella, the 'She-Wolf' of France, was sent to Norfolk by her son, Edward III, in the 14th century to keep her out of the way. Historians now say she was kept in a genteel kind of house arrest, with plenty of freedom to move around, but that hasn't stopped the tales spreading. One says she had a tunnel built from the castle to the Red Mount chapel in Lynn. Entrances have been discovered at both sites, but they were just short passageways. Isabella is also said to haunt Castle Rising. Kings and buried treasure are an important part of folklore. Thetford Castle is a very old site. Occupation dates back to the Iron Age, when it is believed there was a fortification there, while the invading Danes used it as a base during the ninth century. It is said that in ancient times a king once buried a treasure hoard there, covered with an enormous earth mound. In fact, treasure has been discovered nearby, at Gallow's Hill. There is evidence it was Boudica of the Iceni's palace during the 1st century AD. Others say the devil created the castle mound, and you will encounter him if you walk around the castle seven times at midnight. Meanwhile, at Norwich there are almost as many tunnel tales as the city has pubs (or used to, as so many pubs have closed). Another pre-Roman king, named in some legends as Gurgunt, is supposed to be buried underneath the castle hill. There he sits, sword in hand, at a table laden high with gold and silver ornaments. Mound burials were common, and treasures were buried with important people. The discovery of a royal burial site at Sutton Hoo in Suffolk proves this, so there may be something in these stories. In Norwich, the city's cathedral seems to be honeycombed with hidden passages. There was supposed to be one leading to St Benets and another to the nunnery at Carrow; it was there a fat pig entered and got lost. Another passageway is meant to go to the 'Samson and Hercules' building in Tombland, just across the road. The twin statues were reputed to come alive at the stroke of midnight. What we see there now are replicas of the original statues. That of Hercules was removed in 1993. Following renovation, it was installed in pride of place at The Museum of Norwich at The Bridewell in 2019.

What about some hard facts?

Norwich's real tunnels are medieval chalk and flint mines. They were used to extract building materials for the city's buildings and walls up to the 14th century and beyond. They lie between 12ft and 90ft below the surface, varying in height from six to 16ft in height, and six to 12ft in width. In the 19th century mines at Earlham Road were rediscovered, fancy lighting put up and visitors welcomed. Eventually it was realised the tunnels were dangerous, and they were sealed. Subsidence is a problem in parts of Norwich. The city's engineers conduct inspections, and the entrances to the tunnels are kept secret. In 1988 the EDP's picture of a bus which had gone into a hole on Earlham Road went all around the world. Not much buried treasure perhaps – but certainly a world of mystery beneath the surface.

Legend of Saint William

In a corner of Norwich's Mousehold Heath, with the roar of ringroad traffic hard to ignore, is the site of a long forgotten religious house. There's little to see now, but a 900-year-old murder here fuelled anti-Semitic persecution throughout medieval Europe.

Sounds ominous

On Friday, March 23, 1144, the body of a 12-year-old boy was found in woodland outside Norwich. What followed became part of the city's folklore, and made life very difficult for Europe's Jews. It was a monk called Thomas of Monmouth who was largely responsible for inventing the legend of Saint William. Arriving in Norwich a year or two after the boy's body was found, he discovered a legacy of rumour and accusation. Nobody had been found guilty of the crime, and William's family were angry. They believed they knew who the killers were, and the offenders were being shielded by the authorities. With a fertile mind and a determination to create a cult around the story, Thomas wrote a book called The Life and Passion of Saint William. The hero is young William, presented as a saintly boy of Anglo-Saxon peasant stock; the villains are newcomers to Norwich, the Jews.

Convenient scapegoats?

The Jews had arrived in Norwich shortly after the Norman conquest of 1066. As the city prospered and grew, they settled in the area around the castle and marketplace. With a synagogue on White Lion Street, at the foot of Castle Hill, and a population of about 200 people, they were putting down roots. They were welcomed by William the Conqueror for their financial skills, although as moneylenders to landowners and religious bodies they were never going to be universally loved. There was, however, little history of anti-Semitic violence in England before the mid-1100s. The pogroms that afflicted Europe during the first crusade (1095-99) were not repeated here. But rumours were circulating that the Jews hated Christians so much they were poisoning wells, ritually murdering Christian children and drinking their blood at the Passover ceremony. This vindictive fiction, inspired perhaps by fear of outsiders, has become known as the 'blood libel'. One of its earliest manifestations was in Norwich. William came of a respectable family from a village just outside Norwich. Coming to the city, he was apprenticed to a skinner, and through his work came into contact with the city's Jewish community. William disappeared in mysterious circumstances, and his body was found at Thorpe Wood by a man named Henry of Sprowston. Suspicion fell on a Jewish moneylender named Eleazar. When William's uncle Godwin Sturt, a priest, stood up in the cathedral shortly afterwards and accused the Jews of murder, passions were inflamed. Sheriff John de Chesney, the king's representative in Norfolk, intervened by offering the Jews protection – and things seemed to calm down. It was only then that Thomas of Monmouth entered the stage.

What did he say happened?

Thomas visited the scene and interviewed witnesses. William's body had been reburied at the cathedral priory, and tales of miracles happening around his grave were spreading locally. Thomas wrote his version, and alleged the boy was the victim of torture and ritual murder as part of the Jewish Passover. He said the Jews had tricked him to Eleazar's house by offering him work, then gagged, trussed, hung, pierced him in the head and killed him, subsequently drinking his blood. They then hid the body and transported it under cover of darkness outside the city, where they dumped it. Claiming he had been given this information by a Jewish insider, this 'blood libel' spread nationwide and was believed in other parts of the country, with other children allegedy being abducted. Not only did Thomas attack the Jews, he also named those who had 'covered up' the killing – the sheriff and some in the Church establishment. The monk's account is the only substantial source on William's death, so had a massive influence on people.

Any hidden agenda?

We can only guess at Thomas's motives. It is tempting to put a modern twist on his actions and suggest he was trying to promote a cult of Saint William. A cult saint would attract pilgrims to Norwich, and bring wealth and prestige to the priory. Bishop Eborard, in place at the time of William's murder, felt there was no evidence against the Jews but his successor, William de Turbeville, backed Thomas. Events moved on; people were starting to see William in their dreams as his reputation grew. The cult was made official when William was canonised and a shrine set up at the cathedral. A chapel was dedicated to him where his body was found, the scant remains of which can be seen on Mousehold Heath. William was a popular local saint, but his cult didn't spread far beyond Norfolk. Holy Trinity Church, Loddon, has a particularly graphic illustration of his death, painted on a rood screen around 1500, a few decades before his cult was ended by the Reformation. The chapel was dissolved at the same time.

What was the legacy of the legend?

Anti-semitism thrived. By 1189, when Richard I was crowned and announced he was going on crusade, it erupted into bloodshed. At London, York and Lincoln horrible massacres ensued. Jewish businessmen such as Isaac Jurnet, who lived in King Street, Norwich, found themselves at the mercy of the kings to whom they lent money – who exploited them by imprisoning them until they paid money for their release. A century later Edward I gave them the choice of converting to Christianity or leaving the kingdom on pain of death; the most popular thing he ever did. It was only in the mid-1650s that Oliver Cromwell allowed them to return. As for Thomas of Monmouth's tale, it spread throughout the world and has taken a long time to die. In the words of historian Miri Rubin, writing in History Today: "It still resounds in neo-Nazi and some anti-semitic Arab publications." Norwich has little memory now of William, except for an illustrated information board at the chapel site, and the section of the inner ringroad named Saint William's Way.

Return of the saints

In the church known as the Cathedral of the Broads stands a rare survivor of the Catholic Middle Ages – the Ranworth rood screen.

What is a rood screen?

Rood screens were a feature which separated the ordinary congregation's church in the main body of the building – the nave – from the sacred chancel. This was the holy of holies reserved for the clergy beyond, who were held to have a special relationship with the Almighty. In the pre-Reformation church it was an important physical and symbolic boundary between priest and people. Many, such as the screen at Saint Helen's, Ranworth, were lavishly illustrated with pictures of saints and other venerated characters from the Christian pantheon. As impressive as it is, the surviving screen is only part of what would have stood there in the early 1500s. The screen stood below the Great Rood, a depiction of the crucifixion flanked by representations of the Virgin Mary and Saint John. 'Rood' is an old Anglo-Saxon word, meaning 'cross'. A gallery above the screen, reached by a set of steps, but below the crucifixion scene, would have hosted musicians. It is likely the priest would have preached from this same gallery. It was, as church historian Eamon Duffy has written, "a complex icon of the heavenly hierarchy". Much of the fury of the Protestant Reformation was directed against such objects, as they were held to distract people's attention from worshipping God. Reformers also hated the distinction between the clergy and the congregation.

Why is Ranworth so special?

It is unusually complete and of superior quality. The screen fills the chancel arch and extends the full width of the church. Most rood screens were destroyed, if not during the 16th century Reformation then by the more radical Puritan revolution that followed in the 1640s. During and after the civil wars Oliver Cromwell and parliamentary supporters launched a destructive campaign against church decoration. Unlike the rood screen at Binham Priory, near Holt, part of which survived under a layer of whitewash although pulled down from its original position, that at Ranworth has stayed intact. And a remarkable creation it is. A series of 22 individual paintings depicts saints who would have been familiar to a medieval audience steeped in Bible tales. Art historians reckon it dates from the early 1400s, and may have been influenced by technically adept Flemish artists. The technique employed at Ranworth is regarded as superior to that used at most country churches. This implies this community was rich enough to hire an elite practitioner. Most likely a team was at work, with journeymen or apprentices doing the backgrounds and clothing, while the master craftsmen concentrated on the faces.

Who is depicted?

The Twelve Apostles – Jesus's disciples – take up the lower part of the screen. Saint Paul is substituted for Judas Iscariot, who betrayed Christ. Each saint carries a visual emblem by which illiterate people could identify them, but the names are also written on the pictures. Saint Andrew, for example, has the X-shaped cross on which he was martyred. The artist has portrayed each saint against alternating red and green backgrounds. Although each is dressed in rich robes, their feet are bare to emphasise their humility. The Apostles are supplemented on the wings of the screen by figures specific to eastern England. Here is Saint Felix, the bishop who came from France to spread Christianity in East Anglia during the early seventh century. Here also is Saint Etheldreda; an East Anglian princess, she founded the religious house at Ely that survives in cathedral form today as 'The Ship of the Fens'. England's very own Saint George gets a panel to himself. Armoured like a 15th century knight he is seen trampling a dragon underfoot. His sword raised, he is about to deliver the coup de grace while the creature spits defiance at his feet. Saint George's surcoat and shield are decorated with a red cross on a white background; he is the epitome of an English warrior. Opposite him is the Archangel Michael. Sporting a pair of wings, the armoured Michael is also fighting – and beating – a dragon, though this one has seven heads. Other saints include Saint Barbara and Saint Margaret; she too is giving a dragon a hard time, thrusting the staff of a cross into its throat.

We're beginning to feel sorry for the dragons. What did all this symbolise?

Medieval people thought saints interceded between them and God. A prayer to a saint was offered in the hope that his or her influence could be brought to bear. For example, women approaching childbirth prayed to Saint Anne, patron saint of pregnant women. If the paintwork seems a little faded, and the faces of the saints scratched in places, we must remember that church art has a turbulent history. No rood screen survives entirely intact in England. They were initially removed by King Edward VI's Protestant government in 1547, restored by Catholic Mary a decade later, and removed again under her Protestant sister Elizabeth. Reformers covered bare flesh on the paintings, such as faces and feet, with tar as they feared the images would be treated as pagan idols. Paintings that were not destroyed or defaced were whitewashed over. Ironically, as happened at Ranworth, this served to protect the paintings from later iconoclasts during the 1640s intent on removing the last 'Popish superstition' from England. Other examples of paintings can be found in our region at Attleborough, Binham, Blythburgh and Southwold.

Anything else?

Climb nearly 100 narrow, uneven steps and a pair of ladders past the church bells (not as hard as it sounds) and you can access the roof. You'll be rewarded with magnificent views of the Broads as far as the sea, and back towards Norwich. According to legend a monk from nearby St Benets Abbey, Brother Pacificus, was restoring the screen in the 1530s when the monastery was suppressed by Henry VIII. The distraught monk is said to haunt the broad to this day, rowing across at sunset with his little dog for company.

Prophets of doom

In the spring of 1647 William Sedgwick, preacher of the cathedral church at Ely, set out for London. He had important news for the sinful folk of the metropolis; the world was going to end in 14 days. They had better prepare their souls for Christ's imminent arrival.

Off to Speaker's Corner?

Our noble tradition of free speech is something we cherish nowadays, but William Sedgwick and his ilk were not regarded as fringe characters haranguing passers-by. They were in the mainstream of current thinking, and their words were listened to by the highest and lowest in the land. In past times prophecies of the end of the world and the death of kings were regarded as deadly serious. From time to time those in authority saw them as dangerous, and clamped down. The mid-17th century was the heyday of the portentous prophet, but the roots of the tradition go back a long way. Many prophecies hark back to the days of Merlin and the knights of King Arthur. This was a world of ambiguous riddles, with heraldic creatures such as dragons and lions looming large. In the Tudor period they became particularly powerful. The Reformation inspired people to interpret the Bible in their own way, but the authorities were often dismayed by the results they produced. A Norfolk proverb influenced people in the 1540s, with tragic results.

"The country knaves, Hob, Dick and Hick,
With clubs and clouted shoon
Shall fill up Dussindale
With slaughtered bodies soon"

Meaningless verse? Not to Robert Kett's peasant rebels it wasn't. In 1549 they confronted the government in a series of battles in and around Norwich. While they kept to the high ground above the River Wensum, now known as Kett's Hill, they did well. But they met their doom when they took on a professional army of German and Swiss mercenaries hired by the government in August of that year. The blood that soaked Dussindale was Norfolk blood; the rebels died in their thousands. Kett and his brother were among many hanged.

Dangerous words. . .

Elizabethan lawyer and intellectual Sir Francis Bacon dismissed prophecies as good for nothing but "winter talk by the fireside". Others begged to differ. The Duke of Norfolk, for example, was reportedly influenced by a prophecy of a lion (himself) and a lioness (Mary, Queen of Scots) deposing a queen (Elizabeth I). The result; he was executed for plotting the queen's death in 1572. Under the Tudors it became a capital offence to predict the king's death. That may have deterred the sane and sensible – but not everyone came under that category. John Barbour, of Norwich, made a point of telling everyone he met that he had foreseen the king would not live more than three years. Thomas Larke, of Suffolk, proclaimed a white lion would kill the king. They were lucky; the authorities decided they were not worth prosecuting. More prominent people, such as the Maid of Kent, a nun named Elizabeth Barton, were less fortunate. She was executed in 1534 after fortelling Henry VIII's death.

What happened to William Sedgwick?

Born in about 1609, Sedgwick was a Puritan churchman. In the mid-1640s he was known as the Apostle of the Isle of Ely. He was a protege of the Earl of Manchester, and Oliver Cromwell was an admirer. Prophecies of the end of the world were all the rage in the 1640s. The civil wars unleashed all sorts of new ideas. Social unrest caused by conflict created an atmosphere in which religious and political dissidents had a platform on which to broadcast their ideas. The relaxation of previously strict church censorship allowed them to publish widely – for a while at least. Most notable were the Fifth Monarchists. They went back to antiquity to claim that four great monarchies, Babylon, Persia, Greece and Rome, were about to be succeeded by the rule of Christ and his saints. William Sedgwick was of this mindset. Following his mission to warn the sinners of London in March, 1647, ministers interviewed him. Opinions were divided; some thought him "distempered in mind", while others felt "he talks very sensibly". Perhaps it depended on your viewpoint. Sedgwick's later nicknames, Apocalypse Sedgwick and The Spiritual Madman, suggest a certain scepticism among his listeners. You can't help feeling our naturally cynical British sense of humour kicked in when the promised end of the world didn't arrive on time. In 1660 Charles II was restored to the throne, and a conservative reaction began. Sedgwick, by then a more mellow, amenable character, died three years later.

I predict a rather quieter future. . .
Following the Restoration there was a clampdown on freedom of speech (or dangerous fanaticism, depending on your politics) and the world of prophecy went underground. Educated people tended to dismiss it as superstition, though it did not die out entirely. The power of the impending apocalypse retained a little of its potency into the 19th century. It thrived in extreme conditions in societies under pressure. The 1840s in Norfolk fitted the bill. Agricultural depression had thrown many out of work, while the once profitable textile trade of centres such as Norwich was in terminal decline. When two evangelical preachers from the USA arrived in Norfolk in 1844, announcing this wicked world was about to end, many believed, seeing an end to their troubles in such an extreme event. According to one account, "people in Norwich stopped buying potatoes by the sack because the world will be ended before you've finished them".

And today?
Bible-inspired 'End-timers' say the end of the world is just around the corner. Don't laugh. Many of us worried about the Millennium Bug that was going to cause computers to crash and aircraft to fall out of the sky on January 1, 2000. One of my former newspaper colleagues stockpiled tins of baked beans in preparation for the disaster. Maybe William Sedgwick would feel quite at home if he were around today.

Medieval marvels

On the side of the angels. Such church decorations as this angel in Holy Trinity Church, Blythburgh, Suffolk, abounded in medieval East Anglia.

The 'slave queen'

Some years ago a metal detectorist made a fascinating discovery in a field at Postwick, near Norwich. A tiny double-sided gold ring bearing what looked like an erotic drawing has helped solve the puzzle of Bathilde, a seventh century East Anglian slave who became a Frankish queen and a Catholic saint.

An intriguing tale. . .

On one side of the ring there is a fairly rudimentary sketch of a copulating couple. But the other side tells a different tale; it shows the head of a queen with Mathilde's name written in Frankish style as Bathilde. This is a royal seal ring, used to identify and authenticate important letters. The discovery shed new light on a figure whose romantic 'rags to riches' story previously baffled historians. We know little about Mathilde's early life in England, so have to speculate a little. Her name, which means 'Bold In Battle' in old English Anglo-Saxon, places her origins in East Anglia. One version of her story says she was kidnapped as a child by Frankish pirates and sold overseas – an all-too familiar tale of the times. Another says she was an aristocrat, born in about 627AD and possibly a relative of East Anglia's last pagan king, Ricberht. He was a son of Raedwald, the ruler of the Angles who is believed to have been buried in the Sutton Hoo ship unearthed in Suffolk in 1939. In the mid-seventh century what is now England was being governed by Germanic peoples with close links to the continent, and organised into a number of warring kingdoms. East Anglia vied with Wessex, Kent, Northumbria and, above all, with Mercia, for supremacy. The East Anglian ruling house was divided against itself, possibly on religious grounds.

Christian and pagan?

The new religion was gaining converts all the time, particularly among the ruling class. Pagan Ricberht was dethroned in 630 by his Christian brother Sigabert with help from the Franks – the warlike people who had conquered what is now northern France and laid the foundations of that nation state. This was bad news for the young Bathilde. She was sent overseas as a slave, probably as part of the Franks' war booty. Slave trading was a grim, but highly profitable enterprise, and any army would expect to make most of its money by selling on those captured in war and their dependants. Slaves were at the bottom of the hierarchy in Europe at the time, though they could always hope to be freed by a generous master. Whatever the truth of Bathilde's origins, once in France her story is well documented. That said, we have to take all these accounts with a pinch of salt; the main sources are hagiographical stories written by churchmen keen to make her into a saint after her death. They tell a Cinderella-like tale, complete with a prince. She was sent to a part of northern France then called Neustria, near Paris. Clearly a cut above the average slave, and by now a devout Christian, she was soon running the household of a high ranking nobleman, Erchinoald, mayor of the palace of Neustria. Impressed by her beauty and grace, he wanted to marry her after his own wife died. Her clerical biographer tells us she rejected his advances. She cannot have had an aversion to marriage though, for shortly afterwards she met the king.

An offer she couldn't refuse?

Clovis II (Louis in modern French) was the head of the Merovingian dynasty that had ruled much of what is now France and Germany for generations. In 649 he freed and married Bathilde. As the consort of the king she was in a position of power, and used her influence to persuade her husband to ban slavery among Christians (the poor old pagans didn't count). Clovis is presumably the male figure in the drawing on the ring, and it seems this side of the seal was used on private correspondence between the couple. Bathilde bore three sons, Clothaire, Childeric and Thierry, all of whom were to reign. But marriage to a king was no bed of roses. In 656 Clovis died, and Bathilde faced her sternest test. Five-year-old Clothaire became king,

---

but was clearly too young to rule. His mother acted as regent until he came of age. Dark Age kingdoms were violent, unstable places and hard to govern, particularly for a woman. She did a good job for the next decade, protecting the throne, reducing the power of the bishops, strengthening the monasteries, founding hospitals and increasing royal power over the sale of religious relics. She had to be a tough, capable character to achieve this, and some sources say she had a hand in a number of assassinations, including the deaths of bishops. In 665 though, son Clothaire was old enough to rule, and Bathilde retired to a nunnery.

Did she want to go?

"She with great joy shut herself up in this monastery of Chelles, in 665, a happiness which she had long earnestly desired," declares Fr Alban Butler's Life of the Saints. Well. . . perhaps. . . but maybe her sons were tired of mum telling them what to do! Human nature changes very little over the centuries; perhaps Bathilde was happy to relinquish the pressures of government, but it cannot have been easy after ruling a kingdom. In the convent, which she had founded herself, chroniclers say she renounced the trappings of royalty and volunteered to serve the poor and infirm with her own hands. She died at Chelsea, near Paris, in 680, and was canonised by Pope Nicholas I. In France her feast day is January 30, the anniversary of her death. She is patron saint of children, widows and the sick.

How did her ring seal end up in Norfolk?

Good question. It may be that she was in close contact with people in East Anglia; links with northern France were close. Maybe an ambassador to the Angles brought it over, and it was given as a gift to the local aristocracy from the queen. Perhaps it was sent back to her native land after her death. Quite how it ended up in a field is another matter. The full story may remain a mystery, but you can see this extraordinary relic when you visit Norwich Castle Museum's Anglo-Saxon and Viking Gallery.

Stigand the civil servant

He was the last Anglo-Saxon archbishop of Canterbury. A confidante of kings and queens, a powerful politician in a divided England for half a century. And he came from Norwich.

Any connection to the Bayeux Tapestry?

Stigand is pictured in that famous work of art. But it is Norman propaganda rather than English history – for it shows Stigand performing an important symbolic act that in reality was carried out by another. We're getting ahead of ourselves. We really don't know that much about Stigand the man. It appears likely he was from an Anglo-Norse family, and was born, probably in Norwich, in 990, where he and his family are recorded owning land. Danes had settled in East Anglia towards the end of the ninth century, although the area was by then firmly incorporated into the English kingdom. Stigand grew up in troubled times. The Norse raiders had returned, encouraged by the weak reign of Ethelred (The Unready). Norwich and Thetford were attacked by King Sweyn of Denmark in 1004, and Sweyn's son Canute later grabbed the English crown after defeating Ethelred's son Edmund at Ashingdon, Essex. So it comes as a surprise to find an Anglo-Saxon monk in the Danish entourage.

Our man Stigand?

In 1020 he gets his first mention in the Anglo-Saxon Chronicle, the record kept for many years by anonymous English monks. "In this year the king (Canute) went to Ashingdon and had a church built there of stone and lime for the souls of those men who had been slain there, and gave it to his own priest, whose name was Stigand." That Stigand had gone over to the Danes did not make him a traitor; the well-organised Anglo-Saxon clerical bureaucracy supported the new monarch as the legitimate heir to avoid chaos – and most likely helped guide the rough and ready young Viking warrior in kingly duties.

Churchmen were the civil servants of their day, the power behind the throne. Is it too fanciful to imagine Stigand as the 'Sir Humphrey' character from 'Yes Minister', subtly manipulating his royal masters? In time Canute became regarded as a model king, an upholder of law and order and a dutiful son of the Church. Stigand was close to Canute's wife, Queen Emma. She had previously been married to Ethelred and, as the daughter of a Norman Duke, was a powerful character in her own right. Some said Stigand became her lover – but that may have been just malicious gossip. Certainly his career prospered; by 1043 he was Bishop of Elmham in Norfolk. But in that year came the first of many crises. With the death of Canute the throne was contested by various candidates, and eventually came the way of Ethelred's son Edward (the Confessor), who had spent his early life in exile in Normandy. Soon after returning to England he fell out with his mother, and confiscated her lands. In the convoluted royal politics of the 11th century family loyalty was in short supply. Stigand shared her misfortune; he was deprived of his see and possessions.

A serious setback

He soon found new allies. The Godwins were an ambitious Wessex clan who had served under Canute. By the 1040s they were on the rise, and were a serious threat to Edward's crown. Through their influence Stigand was restored to royal favour and also made Bishop of Winchester. Earl Godwin and his sons clashed with the king who, in desperation, banished them. Stigand acted as mediator as the two sides hammered out an uneasy compromise in 1052. As part of the bargain many of the Norman churchmen who had accompanied Edward from his exile when he became king were sent packing. Among them was Robert de Jumiéges, Archbishop of Canterbury. Stigand was duly appointed to the top job. The see of Canterbury was as high as an English churchman could go. Although holding two sees constituted an offence in church law, it was commonplace. Churchmen like Stigand became wealthy by holding several positions. It was frowned upon by the Pope in Rome though, with dire consequences for the future. The papacy saw the English Church as corrupt and 'schismatic', and acted against it. Stigand was excommunicated for this pluralism. The Anglo-Saxon Chronicle for 1053 noted: "In this year there was no lawful archbishop in this land, though Stigand occupied the see of Canterbury in Christ Church." An academic issue, you may think. But it was ammunition for ambitious would-be invaders to use in a war of words against England. In Normandy, Duke William would in the next decade enlist the aid of the pope in Rome to support his invasion plans, helping him raise troops and gain vital allies. Stigand's position was further undermined when the deposed "Anti-Pope" Benedict authorised his appointment; it was more ammunition for his critics. On the death of the childless King Edward the Confessor, Harold Godwin became king. In the Bayeux Tapestry it is Stigand pictured crowning Harold – but in reality, the king made sure Bishop Ealdred of York carried out the ceremony; he knew Stigand was compromised and wanted his coronation to be as uncontroversial as possible. That cut no ice with Duke William; his army sailed for England.

1066 and all that

It may have appeared at first to the English clergy that William the Conqueror would be another Canute, a malleable ruler who would leave things as they wanted them. Stigand submitted quickly to the Norman after the defeat and death of Harold at Hastings in 1066 – and took the rest of the church and royal administration with him. This helped legitimise the new regime, and ensure the government of the country passed smoothly on. William was crowned at Westminster Abbey. But he was no Canute. Ruthlessly, the Conqueror changed the face of England forever, bringing in his own people – and there was no room for slightly dodgy English clergymen with enemies in Rome. The vultures circled. Stigand was rather conveniently accused of simony – the buying and selling of church offices. In 1070, William discarded him and appointed a Norman in his place. Stigand had used up the last of his nine lives. He was imprisoned, his property confiscated by the Crown, and he died two years later at Winchester.

Guthrum the Viking

Ah, the Vikings. Longships, pillage, horned helmets . . .

There's no place in this story for horned helmets. And calling them Vikings is not strictly correct. Guthrum, East Anglia's ruler in the late 9th century, was an aristocratic Dane. He could have turned the whole of Britain into a Scandinavian province had he not been beaten back by arguably England's greatest king. Guthrum's life coincided with one of the most violent periods in our history. His influence, and that of his people who settled in East Anglia, helped shape the country we live in today.

No horned helmets then?

Sadly, this image of the Vikings is probably a myth to make them more terrifying. Historians find no evidence they wore them. Guthrum enters the tale just as the last Anglo-Saxon king of East Anglia exits. Norsemen from Denmark, Norway and Sweden had been raiding the shores of Britain for several generations when, in the second half of the ninth century, they began to settle the lands they conquered. Technically, the word Viking is an activity – to go a-viking was to go raiding overseas; the people who began overrunning England from 865 onwards were Danes. There are several theories explaining their explosion onto the world stage. One is that overpopulation and scant resources in Scandinavia spurred their exploits, another is that technological advances in shipbuilding made long distance voyages possible. Perhaps it was just an aggressive spirit of adventure and individualism that led adventurous Scandinavians to these shores, as well as an impressive string of conquests in Ireland, France, Russia and the Mediterranean from the eighth to 11th centuries. Their illiterate society left few written records, so our main sources are churchmen. As they were the victims of the pagan Vikings' raids of plunder it is no surprise they hated them. Anglo-Saxon England was a tempting target;

divided into warring kingdoms – Northumbria, Wessex, Mercia, Kent and East Anglia – and among the richest countries in western Europe, it was no surprise the northmen coveted England's treasures. The first descents on the coastline were for plunder; then the Danes came to stay.

Did no-one try to stop them?
Although their numbers were few they had advantages of surprise, the mobility afforded by their command of the sea – and their ferocity. Modern scholars try to paint the Vikings as traders and craftsmen; they may well have been, but the men who made up Guthrum's army were tough, ruthless fighters. He was a powerful earl who, the sagas say, had killed the king of Denmark in 865. His name does not figure in the first wave of invaders. They were led by the enigmatically named Ivar the Boneless and his brothers, and in 867 they seized Northumbria. Two years' later it was East Anglia's turn. King Edmund was defeated, probably at Thetford, and martyred. Guthrum arrived on the scene with a second wave of Danish settlers. With the Mercian midlands largely in Norse hands by now only Wessex – south-western and southern England – and its young king held out. In the nick of time England found a hero. Alfred rallied his forces to face the Danes, now led by Guthrum, as they headed west. He beat them in a desperate battle fought at Ashdown, Berkshire, in 871, which won him some time. He paid off the Danes with gold to buy a little more breathing space. Guthrum based himself at Cambridge as his Danes put down roots in this region. Soon he was on the march. By 878, following a surprise attack during the Christmas celebrations, he was close to victory. Alfred was pinned down in the Somerset marshes fighting a guerrilla campaign and Guthrum's hold on Wessex tightened. At the eleventh hour, Alfred raised a new army and beat the Danes in a pitched battle at Edington, Wiltshire. Guthrum surrendered. Surprisingly, Alfred spared his life in return for his conversion to Christianity. England was partitioned; the north and east became the Danelaw, as it was there the Danes settled. It was a temporary truce in

an ongoing war, but Guthrum ruled in East Anglia until his death in 890. Archaeologists have found evidence of an upsurge in urban life under the Danes. Norwich, previously a collection of Saxon settlements, began to take shape. We can see this in place names; the Danish -gate suffix features in Fishergate, Colegate, Pottergate and Cowgate, and Thorpe, as in Thorpe St Andrew, is the Danish word for settlement. Look also for the Scandinavian -by ending in names such as Scratby and Hemsby.

What sort of king was Guthrum?

With Alfred as his godfather, and adopting the baptismal Christian name Athelstan, Guthrum began to appear rather 'English', even minting his own coins. The Danes were probably relatively few in number, a few thousand at most, replacing the English elite. Anglo-Saxons and Scandinavians had much in common, having been connected by trade and cultural links for centuries. The Danes assimilated, replacing love of war with devotion to land and trade. Their domination of East Anglia ended within two decades of Guthrum's death. Alfred's warrior successors reconquered the region south of the Humber by 917 – ending its independence forever – and used it as a springboard to unite the country. We had not seen the back of the Vikings. In 1004 Sweyn of Denmark ravaged Norwich and Thetford on the way to making his son Canute king of England. As late as 1070 a Viking fleet allied – rather unreliably – with fenland hero Hereward the Wake against the Normans, helping themselves to the treasures of Peterborough cathedral. Old habits died hard.

What was the Danish legacy in the east of England?

Danes stayed on as farmers and traders in eastern England. They had laid down roots that proved strong in the long run. Although their influence was strongest in the north, it's tempting to see a streak of stubborn Norse belligerence in Norfolk's enduring 'do-different' attitude. Archaeologists continue to search for our Viking heritage. Maybe one day they'll discover a horned helmet. . .

Making Yarmouth Great

At first there was just a sand bar, thrown up by the sea. Then came the fishermen, followed by the church. Great Yarmouth grew from nothing into a mighty medieval port.

Shifting sands of history?

The North Sea shapes our coastline. To an extent we are all becoming more aware of, climate change and the vagaries of the sea in the form of coastal erosion and the power of nature may decide our future in this part of the world. It certainly decided our past. Yarmouth was created and formed by the ocean. When the Romans came to Britain in the 1st Century AD, what is now the east coast of Norfolk looked very different to how it is now. Great Yarmouth did not exist. Instead, a vast open estuary extended from Caister south to Burgh, and inland as far as what are now Acle and Reedham, which stood on slightly higher dry land. This estuary branched into the rivers Yare, Bure and Chet. The Romans built forts to guard the estuary at Caister and Burgh, and imported and exported goods from ports along its shores to their East Anglian capital at Venta Icenorum, now Caistor St Edmund, near Norwich. It was not until several centuries later that a sand bar gradually rose at the eastern edge of this estuary. The Saxon Saint Fursey set up a religious community nearby, probably at the site of the now crumbling Roman fort at Burgh in about 640AD. The sand bar, meanwhile, became a narrow island, some eight miles in length, from north to south.

Right. Nice seaside beaches, good views. . .

Medieval people had little interest in such things. Life was tough. Few people had time to take a holiday on the coast, and anyway, wasn't that where marauding pirates and invaders were likely to land and cause havoc? What attracted interest was something far more useful from the sea. Fish. To be precise, herrings. These little 'silver darlings' were to become all-important. Gathering in huge shoals they could be found up and down the coast of the British Isles for much of the year, from Scotland in early summer, along the north coast of England in mid-summer, and off East Anglia from September or October until December. Travelling fishermen followed the herrings' course for much of the year, and the sand bar island eventually became the site for temporary housing during the season. Following trade came the church. A small chapel, dedicated to St Benet, was also occupied during the herring season. From the 10th century onwards, the British climate became warmer, and population grew. When the northern channel silted up, the sand island became a peninsula. Modern Yarmouth was born, and became prosperous.

Why?

Fish was important in the medieval period. During Christian fasts when meat was unavailable, it became a popular alternative. Herring was particularly useful as, when packed in salt, it would last longer than many alternatives. Some historians believe it was the Danish invaders – Vikings – who popularised a fish diet. At all events, the little settlement of Yarmouth grew quickly, as smoking, salting and drying of the herring turned into a major industry. From as few as five houses on the shore in about 1000 (which were destroyed by King Sweyn's Viking forces in 1004 when they attacked East Anglia) Yarmouth became significant enough to attract the attention of royalty. By 1041 it belonged to the king himself, Edward the Confessor. The Domesday Book four decades later recorded 70 burgesses, 24 fishermen belonging to the manor of Gorleston – and a population of about 400 people. The town looked inland, towards the river rather than sea. This, apparently, was because the fishermen wanted to avoid the salt spray from the ocean. Yarmouth was sandwiched into a narrow area between sea and river, a factor which would soon lead to serious overcrowding.

When did Yarmouth become Great?

The term Great Yarmouth was originally coined to differentiate the main town from Little Yarmouth, on the west bank of the Yare, which became Southtown. The title continued in use to avoid confusion with Yarmouth, Isle of Wight. Yarmouth also proved an attractive port for shipping. The coast was protected by sand banks three miles out to sea. These 'Yarmouth roads' offered safe passage to ships, as did a lack of rocks on which to founder. But it was the fish that paid the bills. The 'silver darlings' were collected in 'lasts' of 10,000 and 'crans', baskets which could hold up to 1,500 fish – some indication of the scale of the industry. By the early 1200s fish were so ubiquitous that "in whole or part payment of debts, Yarmouth paid in herrings". As Yarmouth was a royal possession, King Henry I put it under the rule of an official called a reeve in 1100. But it was a powerful churchman who had the greatest influence. Herbert de Losinga had already begun building Norwich Cathedral and founded the port of Lynn when he turned his attention to Yarmouth in 1101. He demolished tiny St Benets Church, and ordered construction of a new one. By the time this new church, dedicated to St Nicholas, patron saint of fishermen, was complete in 1119, Yarmouth was a major town. Its huge marketplace also evolved, and has been in constant use for more than 800 years. By now an entrepot for the growing metropolis of Norwich, limestone bound for the building of the city's castle and cathedral was unloaded at Yarmouth, and sent off inland by river.

Any ups and downs?
As the harbour entrance kept silting up, it had to be moved several times – a constant factor on this coastline. The south coast Cinque Ports claimed jurisdiction over Yarmouth's fishermen, leading to friction and sporadic violence at sea. As the Middle Ages drew on, the Royal Navy became more important to the town. Yarmouth was in the front line during the Hundred Years War with France. Norfolk seamen such as Sir John Perebrowne distinguished themselves in battle, and the citizens began work on building defensive walls. King John recognised the town's importance by granting it a Charter in 1208, allowing it some self-government. Yarmouth had really become Great.

Norfolk's 'inland' ports

The north Norfolk coastline is an area of great natural beauty, popular with nature lovers and walkers. But why are the former ports of the area set so far back from today's coastline? The answer comes from both natural and man-made causes. It shows how history can leave a thriving place high and dry.

Hard to imagine them as anything but quaint and cosy. . .
There was a time, in the Middle Ages, when the Blakeney Haven area – comprising Blakeney, Cley and Wiveton – was a hive of activity. Blakeney was once in the top 10 of British harbours, the ports made a vital contribution in time of war, while smugglers rubbed shoulders with fighting men, fishermen and merchants. Today these places are busy again – but it is tourists, bird-watchers, walkers and second-homers who are drawn to this coastline. But when the River Glaven was navigable from the sea, ocean-going vessels docked at the harbours of these three places, as well as at other sites along this stretch of coast, such as Stiffkey and Salthouse. Although Wiveton appears to be well inland, grooves on the side of the church indicate that ships once used it to moor up.

Who founded the ports?
One legend says the Vikings were the first to use Blakeney harbour more than a thousand years ago. Certainly, by the 14th century, it was an important place. East Anglia looked out to sea, as much as it did inland. In 1347 the port provided ships for King Edward III's siege of Calais at the start of the Hundred Years War and they were present at the English victory at the Battle of Sluys, off Flanders. Two centuries later, when the Spanish Armada threatened invasion, Blakeney, Cley and Wiveton mustered an impressive 36 ships for the navy. It was Cley mariners who, in 1405, captured the heir to the throne of Scotland while en route to France; he was held in England as a hostage for

several years. But it was peaceful trade that built the prosperity of these ports. Blakeney was one of the few ports allowed to trade in silver, gold and horses, while coal from Newcastle came in here. Stone quarried in Northamptonshire was brought up by river and sea to build some of Norfolk's great houses and churches. The ports were embarkation points for locally grown wheat and for wool products, the foundation of English wealth during the later Middle Ages. The harbours were lined with wharves, and would have been teeming with activity and the sound of many languages. Norfolk's close links with the Netherlands and northern France are reflected throughout the region. As our closest trading partners, influences from the Low Countries prevail – the Dutch gables on many of the buildings the most obvious examples. Daring East Anglian fishermen went out as far as Iceland from the 16th century onwards.

What about the smugglers?

As early as 1317, Cley harbour was supposedly run by gangs of organised pirates. Smuggling was never eradicated, despite the best efforts of the authorities. At Cley an impressive Customs and Excise building was later erected which was in use until the second half of the 19th century. Blakeney's Crown and Anchor inn was said to be a hotbed of smuggling and general nefarious activities; it was demolished in 1921 to make way for the Blakeney Hotel. Legends persist of a network of tunnels used by local villains to transport contraband.

And legitimate traders?

Merchants founded an impressive flowering of building. St Nicholas' Church at Blakeney, built on the foundations of a 13th century Carmelite friary, is still a landmark on high ground that can be seen for miles across the salt marshes. In the marshes, on the Blakeney to Cley coastal walk, are the remains of another friary. Merchant vessels and fishermen would stop there for a blessing to bring good luck to their voyage. At Wiveton the builders of St Mary's Church put the richest flush work ornamentation on the side of the church that faces Cley to impress the neighbours. Blakeney Guildhall, complete with 15th century undercroft, was probably the house of a well-off fish merchant. Salthouse, by contrast, featured warehouses to store salt from the marshes. As late as the 17th century this was a busy, working coastline.

Where did it all go wrong?

Nature and man took a hand. The north Norfolk coast is at right angles to the prevailing tide, acting as a natural groyne. Spits and sandbars form easily, silting goes on and saltmarsh forms. This eventually blocked the course of the river, and cut the villages off from the coast so they are a mile or more inland. At Stiffkey the harbour where materials used to build Sir Nathaniel Bacon's great hall arrived in 1578 eventually became unusable – and the process spread along the coastline. Wealthy landowners such as Sir Henry Calthorpe speeded up what was happening naturally. Despite warnings and legal protests, he persisted in draining salt marsh for agricultural use. In 1637 he put a dam across the Glaven and enclosed the marshes. Although the bank was later demolished, the river channel had already began to silt up. Soon ships could not get to the Cley wharves; it was no longer "by-the-sea". Trade continued along the coast, but the good times were over. The failure to attract the railway in the 1840s was the final blow. By the 1850s even the smugglers were struggling, the Cley customs house closed in 1853 and the economy slumped. Unemployment rose, and there were slums in Blakeney as living conditions deteriorated.

Not for long. . .

Increasing national wealth and leisure time during the second half of the 19th century brought tourists. In 1926 the Norfolk Naturalists Trust (now the Norfolk Wildlife Trust) bought 400 acres of marshland between Cley and Salthouse, and nature lovers flocked to the area. Nature and human interference continue to influence this fragile coast; concerns over flooding, climate change, erosion and over-development mean its course remains as shifting as a sandbar.

The walled city

Norwich city walls are there for all driving around the inner ring road to see. Hard to believe that these strange heaps of rubble left over from the Middle Ages once stood at least 12ft high, and were the pride of England's second city.

They go on for miles

In a circuit stretching from Carrow around Norwich, interrupted on one side by the River Wensum, the city walls contained an area 1½ miles north to south and one mile east to west. From the 1300s they defined the city, with a number of gates marking strategic entry and exit points for the best part of 500 years. When celebrated traveller Celia Fiennes visited Norwich in 1698 she remarked on the "vast place" within two and a half miles of walls. Norwich had come a long way from the Anglo-Viking settlement known as Northwic. This had grown up from what is now the Tombland area of the city, and expanded either side of the river. The Danes who came in the late ninth century made a great contribution to its growth, one that archaeologists are still investigating. It may have been them who created Norwich's first line of defences – an earth bank thrown up around a far smaller area than the later walls.

Were they any good?

These defences were breached in 1004. In that year Sweyn of Denmark sacked both Norwich and Thetford; we don't know what kind of resistance was mounted. On two further occasions Norwich suffered the indignity of capture. In 1174 Flemish mercenaries fighting against Henry II sacked the town, and less than 40 years later King Louis of France seized it, during the disastrous reign of King John. The citizens clearly decided that enough was enough. By now Norwich was a growing and prosperous place. King Richard had granted it a charter in 1194, and from this date its status as a city was guaranteed. Its

Parts of the once formidable medieval city walls survive in Norwich, an intriguing sight for motorists doing battle with the inner ring road. Here is a section in the St Stephens area of the city, near the main bus station.

inhabitants' decision to pay for and construct the walls demonstrated their civic pride. After much planning and fundraising, work finally began in 1297. A bank was made with material from the existing ditch and a further structure set on top. Not everyone was happy – the new ditch cut through church land, which led to conflict between city and priory. The walls were made of flint and mortar, which were used in huge quantities. The whole circuit took half a century to complete, and when done it could boast more than 40 towers and 12 fortified toll gates: King Street, Ber Street, Brazen Gate, St Stephen's, St Giles's, St Benedict's, Heigham Gate, and, on the north side of the river, St Martin's, St Augustine's, Magdalen Gate and Pockthorpe Gate. Bishop's Bridge Gate controlled the river crossing, complete with a gatehouse on the bridge. At the southern end, where the wall met the river at Carrow, boom towers were created and a chain of iron laid into the water, defending the city from water-borne attack.

Who paid for this?

Most was contributed by private citizens. Norwich had a population estimated at 30,000, making it England's second city, but its walls were greater in length than those of London and Southwark combined. One wealthy Norwich man, Richard Spynk, paid from his own pocket. His reward was exemption from taxes and tolls for him and his descendants. By 1343, when the walls were complete, they covered the inhabited area of the city on both sides of the river, excluding the suburb of Heigham, a village in its own right. There was one blind spot; where the meandering Wensum snaked around the city no walls were built. Instead a large fortress, now known as Cow Tower, was created later in the 14th century. The French never returned, but that was not to say there was always peace. In 1266 a group of rebel barons, fighting against the rule of Henry III and nominally loyal to Simon de Montfort, looted the city, while during the 1381 Peasants' Revolt, Geoffrey Lister's insurgents wreaked havoc. The most serious threat to the city came from Kett's Rebellion of 1549 (of which you can read more later in this book). Estimated at 10,000 strong, Robert Kett's Norfolk rebels camped outside the walls, up from the river on Mousehold Heath. Their attack came at the weak point – across the river – and the fiercest fighting took place at the still standing Bishop Bridge. Cow Tower was bombarded from the heights by captured artillery. Initially the royal troops were routed, and the rebels briefly held the city before being crushed by reinforcements.

Did the walls lead to cramped conditions in the city?

Being so large the walls allowed for several centuries of unimpeded growth. Although the poor lived cheek by jowl, the wealthy elite had space to create spacious gardens and orchards for themselves. But by the 18th century the walls and gates had become a hindrance to traffic. They were an expensive irrelevance as Norwich was growing both within and without the walls. There were no heritage societies or conservation groups to campaign to save them. By 1791 they were denounced as "a nuisance that smells rank in the nose of modern improvement". From 1790 to 1810 the corporation demolished the gates. Sketches made by artists of the contemporary Norwich School, such as John Sell Cotman, show the gates in their latter days, more ramshackle than romantic. As the walls fell into disuse housing grew up within and without, often cannibalising the materials, while much perished as roads were built and widened. The south side of St Benedict's Street Gate survived until 1942, complete with a doorpin. It fell victim to bombing during the Second World War 'Baedecker Raids' which devastated the city.

What's left today?

A total of 15 sections survive above ground, including the ruined Cow Tower by the river. To name a few, large parts remain at St Stephens, Chapelfield, where you can see evidence of arrow loops, at Carrow Road, near the football ground, the junction of Magpie Road and Magdalen Street where the gate once stood and at Barrack Street. At St Stephens a fine mural illustrates the gate in its glory days, when the city welcomed Queen Elizabeth I during her summer 1578 Progress throughout East Anglia. If you want to see what the walls may have looked like in their heyday, visit the city of Chester, where the medieval walls have, miraculously, survived into the 21st century. There have been a few archaeological digs in Norwich, most notably during the 1950s at Barn Road, but the walls retain much of their air of mystery and romance to a modern viewer.

Capital of East Anglia

In 1066 it was the sixth largest town in England, an industrial hub of Norfolk – and the capital of East Anglia.

Right, that's Norwich then. . .

Not quite. In the middle of the 11th century the honour went to Thetford. Two centuries of rapid growth had seen the population soar, manufacturing take off, domestic and overseas trade links forged and religious houses moving in and setting up churches and abbeys. Dominating its agricultural hinterland, providing a market for produce, and sitting on top of a crossroads linking the routes east to west, and north to south, things couldn't be better for this town on the Norfolk-Suffolk border. But, just as its golden age was getting into full swing, Thetford was about to go into a steep decline following the Norman Conquest of 1066.

Those rotten Normans!

Actually, it wasn't their fault. A combination of shifting economic fortunes and a bitter dispute between bishops and abbots meant Thetford lost its eminent position within the span of a generation. But we're getting ahead of ourselves. The settlement of Thetford went back to Iron Age times, when the Iceni built a hillfort and ceremonial buildings, which may have been Boudica's palace. There is evidence of continual settlement through Roman times into the arrival of the Anglo-Saxons. It was largely rural, and there are few signs of a town. The first Saxon settlement grew from what was called the Red Castle, some way from the old hillfort site. Rapid development and building following the Second World War has eradicated most of the archaeological remains, so the full story of Thetford's rise cannot be told. The Red Castle was fortified with earthworks, and it had a church dedicated to St Lawrence. The town grew rapidly in the two centuries after 850AD. This was down to trade and transport. Its position as a transport crossroads made it an ideal place for trade, and the growth of the pottery industry provided employment. The river port at Thetford saw goods such as grain, wool and timber sent for export overseas. By the time of the Viking invasions Thetford was a significant centre in the kingdom of East Anglia. As we have seen, the Danish army, under Ivar 'the Boneless' Lothbroksson, defeated East Anglia's King Edmund in 869 at Hoxne, in Suffolk. After executing the king the Danes used Thetford as a base. They ruled East Anglia until defeated by the resurgent English in 917. Their influence on Thetford is enigmatic. Did Danish merchants improve trade links with Scandinavia, as it is suggested they did in Norwich? Certainly, the Danish invasion did not hamper the town's meteoric growth. By 1000 there was a growing artisans' quarter, as the pottery business boomed. 'Thetford' ware was modelled on German pottery. Tanners thrived elsewhere in the town, woollen goods were produced, and suburbs mushroomed beyond the town walls. When the Viking incursions began again, in the 990s, the town's defences were improved. They did not help much when Denmark's King Sweyn sacked the town in 1004 (he had already seen to Norwich). This was despite the best efforts of East Anglia's ealdorman (earl) Ulfcetel 'the Valiant'. He caught up with the Danes and fought them to a standstill, winning their respect, but was ultimately thwarted at a battle near Thetford. "All the flower of the East Anglian people perished," mourned the Anglo-Saxon Chronicle.

Bad for trade?
Despite this setback, and another English defeat at Thetford six years later, the town's growth continued. Sweyn's son, Canute, seized the English crown. Surprisingly, perhaps, it turned out to be Thetford's most prosperous time. Canute proved an able ruler, and England's position as part of an Anglo-Scandinavian empire boosted trade – particularly for towns in reach of the east coast. By the mid-11th century the population had risen to 4,500, a figure it would not reach again until the 1950s. A total of 14 pre-1066 churches have been identified, and the town ranked level with Norwich, Lincoln and

Oxford, while York and London were the two greatest cities in England. Thetford was the site of a royal mint, with half a dozen coin producers at work. Granted the status of a borough, it had certain self-governing rights over property which gave it another advantage. In the immediate aftermath of the Norman Conquest, it seemed the town's informal position as East Anglia's capital would continue. William the Conqueror replaced Aethelmar, the English Bishop of East Anglia, with his own man – Herfast. He switched his seat from North Elmham to Thetford, and created a cathedral there which would later house the Dominican abbey. People in this boom town probably sat back and expected the good times to roll.

Things are never that easy. . .

A rapid decline set in. Trade competition from places such as Lynn, Ely, Bury St Edmunds and Norwich undermined Thetford's economy. These centres were backed by powerful churchmen; Herbert de Losinga at Lynn and Norwich, and Bury by its abbot. Thetford's chief landowner, Roger Bigod, took little interest in the town. When the powerful abbot of Bury, keen to see his town prosper and get one up on the Bishop of East Anglia, started throttling neighbouring Thetford's trade by regulating who could sell what and where, the town suffered from its lack of a powerful patron. The pottery industry collapsed, and the population fell by a quarter to 3,600 by 1086. The bishop took note, and moved his see from Thetford to Norwich in 1094. Even the farmers moved on, sheep and rabbit farming replacing labour-intensive arable farming in the Brecks. It seems the sandy soil was exhausted, so crops failed. A temporary motte and bailey castle, thrown up by the Normans in the aftermath of the Conquest on the site of the Iceni fort, was not made permanent. It was demolished following a rebellion in 1173. The Norman castle created at Norwich, by contrast, developed into the imposing structure we see today, followed by the cathedral. Norwich got what Thetford might have had. The town became a backwater, and remained so until post Second World War expansion.

As old as the Adam. . .

In 1249 an army of stonemasons was working on Norwich Cathedral. They were thirsty. They were hungry. Supply met demand. . . and the Adam and Eve public house emerged to meet their needs. Since then generations of drinkers have stepped into this characterful little gem of a pub. It is, as the sign tells us, probably the oldest pub in Norwich (unless you know better. . .)

People have been drinking there for 750 years

Probably longer. In Anglo-Saxon times there was a well underneath what is now the lower bar, the oldest surviving part of the pub. Recorded history begins in 1249. Those cathedral workers were the first recorded customers, when they were paid with bread and ale. Monks from the Great Hospital, just down the road, were the first owners of the pub. They were known as great beer brewers, strictly for medicinal purposes, you know. In those days before we had drinks like tea and coffee, water that was home to harmful bacteria could be too dangerous to drink. People drank 'small' beer for their health – particularly children. This had a low alcohol content, typically below 1 per cent ABV, and was nutritional. The monks added living accommodation and the familiar Flemish-style gables. In the summer of 1578, during Queen Elizabeth I's grand visit to Norwich, she passed by the pub during a procession to a torch-lit pageant on the nearby River Wensum. We'd like to think she popped in for a cheeky half. . . Since those days the Adam has been home to an assortment of characters; from clergy to smugglers, from cathedral choristers to a notorious murderer or two. It even has two recorded ghosts.

Where did they get their beer?

In medieval times it was always brewed on the premises. Many women had the job. For example, the famous traveller Margery Kempe, of Lynn, was that town's biggest brewer in the early 1400s. Up until fairly modern times the tradition of the 'ale wife' was maintained. Norwich was always known for its pubs; at one time the saying was "a pub for every day of the week and a church for every week of the year". Sadly, those days are long gone.

The Adam and Eve. Probably the oldest pub in Norwich.

What about those ghosts?

The spectre of one of the medieval French-speaking monks supposedly buried beneath the floorboards in the lower bar has been glimpsed. Far more famous is 'Sam'. This friendly ghost is that of Lord Sheffield. When Robert Kett's rebels burst across the Bishop Bridge in the summer of 1549, his Lordship was among the fighters tasked to stop them. In the running battles that erupted along this part of the Norwich riverside, Sheffield was among the casualties. His men took the mortally wounded man to the Adam and Eve, where he died. Regulars to this day claim his ghost occasionally makes off with a coat or scarf – usually returned the next day – or taps you on the shoulder. There is no cause for alarm. Today the pub is the starting and finishing point for the popular city ghost walks.

And the smugglers?

Mid-19th century landlady Elizabeth Howes owned a wherry, which bore her name, and in which she brought in sacks of sand from Great Yarmouth. She sold this to pubs for their floors and spitoons, but the sacks also reputedly contained illicit liquor. In those days of high import duties many people avoided paying by this kind of smuggling. Howes apparently did a roaring trade in contraband. Customers at this time included literary giants such as George Borrow, the author of Romany Rye. They rubbed shoulders with low life. In 1848 farmer James Blomfield Rush, said to be a pub regular, murdered the Recorder of Norwich, Isaac Jermy and his son. It was said he planned the deed over a beer at the pub. After his conviction a crowd of several thousands watched him hanged at Norwich Castle the following April. This was not the first such brush with death; in 1800 a killing was committed near the pub in the grounds of the Great Hospital; after confessing the killer was also executed.

Thank goodness, the licensees were all such upstanding characters! As society became more ordered, the late 19th century police force started asking awkward questions. Large locked gates prevented them from supervising the pub in the early hours, and the Chief Constable of Norwich opposed the renewal of the Adam's licence at the 1905 court sessions. Only by agreeing not to lock the gates were the licensees allowed to carry on serving. During the First World War, the 1915 Defence of the Realm Act introduced the strict licensing regime which was only relaxed in the early years of this century. Two licensees of the pub – John and Sophia Andrews – were convicted in 1915 and 1920 of allowing consumption out of hours; the punishment was a £1 fine or 13 days' detention. The Adam and Eve was said to be the last Norwich pub to serve "from the wood" – ie straight from the barrel. It was not until 1973 that the first bar was installed. Its position near the law courts ensures a colourful clientele, including the police, legal profession and their clients as well as local journalists. It is very much on the tourist trail, as well as a magnet for loyal regulars. Recent celebrity visitors have included the late actor Sir John Hurt, Olympian Dame Kelly Holmes, political activist Peter Tatchell, dancer Wayne Sleep, former frontman of the Undertones Feargal Sharkey and comedian Vic Reeves, while regulars include Norfolk 'pop' artist Colin Self. Licensee Rita McCluskey has been at the pub since 2001. She sees staff and customers alike as a continuation of the long line of characters who make pubs the heart of their community. Long may it continue.

Marshland cathedrals

Isolated and underpopulated, despised by contemporaries, the marshlands of west Norfolk and Lincolnshire produced stunning medieval churches. Many of them look as ornate as cathedrals.

Why were they built?

A complex mix of genuine faith and expression of wealth. Surely there must also have been an element of getting one up on the neighbours. From the time of the Norman Conquest in 1066 to the 16th century these islands of civilisation in an otherwise hostile terrain produced exquisite churches. Set in a rough arc about ten miles wide between Wisbech and King's Lynn, those at Walsoken, West Walton, Walpole St Andrew, Walpole St Peter, Terrington St John and Terrington St Clement stand out. Not forgetting the gem just over the Lincolnshire border at Long Sutton. Even today, on back roads sliced off between the A47 and A17 trunk roads, these villages have an otherworldly feel to them. Imagine how they felt during the medieval period. Cut off by trackless marshland and fen, many of the fenmen made a precarious living by catching fish and wildfowl. The 17th century antiquarian John Camden described the 'fen tigers' as "a kind of people according to the nature of the place they dwell, rude, uncivil and envious to all others". To which the tough and independent fenmen no doubt would give a firm response! It was near Walpole St Andrew that King John's treasure, according to legend, went under the water in 1216, never to be found again. Today the church still houses a shrine for travellers, a relic of the days when marsh travel was precarious. You would have needed an experienced guide to see you safely through the marshes, subject as they were to sudden tides and rushing water. The fens provided a (probably) mythical hero named Tom Hickathrift, the slayer of giants in the marshes. At Walpole St Peter a supporting figure in the external brickwork is said to represent Hickathrift, who is buried in the churchyard at his native Tilney All Saints, if you believe the stories. It is possible Hickathrift was a local strong man who rid the marshland of bandits and offered protection to local people. From these unpromising surroundings, people produced churches praised as 'cathedrals'.

They must have been expensive to build. Who was paying?

Sheep. Well, not literally. During the Middle Ages England's economy was largely based on its prodigious wool exports. Not for nothing did the Lord Chancellor sit on a woolsack at Westminster. Even today two pubs in Norwich are named The Woolpack in honour of that trade. Links to the Low Countries were provided through the growing ports of Lynn and Wisbech to the north, Yarmouth to the east and places such as Ipswich to the south of East Anglia. The trade culminated during the 16th century when cities in Flanders such as Antwerp were full of English merchants. There was two-way traffic. Many skilled Flemish and French textile workers found their way to England, particularly to cities like Norwich, where they were known as the 'Strangers'. The Flemish influence is abundant in the marshland churches. At Terrington St John a fine carving of the Archangel Gabriel is of 15th century Flemish design, while at St Peter a wooden chancel screen depicts St Gudela carrying a model of Brussels cathedral, the city of which she was patron saint.

When were they built?

Walsoken All Saints is the oldest, the earliest parts dating from 1146 though, like all churches, it has been added to and amended over the centuries. It has been described as "the grandest Norman church in Norfolk". At West Walton, the Church of St Mary the Virgin was begun in about 1240. Hailed as an example of early English style, it was built of Barnack stone and has a detached bell tower. Prominent landowner William de Warenne and the Bishop of Ely were moving spirits behind the construction. Built at the end of the 14th century Terrington St Clement is named after an early pope, and is called the "Cathedral of the Marshlands". Its detached north west tower is 87ft high, which came in handy in 1670 when villagers took refuge from yet more floods. Although Terrington St John dates from 1423 it seems likely an earlier church stood on the spot. Similarly, St Peter's tower was built in 1300. It survived flooding 37 years later that washed away the rest of the church. Walpole St Andrew was rebuilt between 1440 and 1520.

Any special features?

St Peter's is a beautiful building. Its austere interior has a wooden nave screen built in the 1630s. A unique feature is the 'Bolt Hole', a passage probably built to preserve an ancient right of way, the origin of which is unknown. Carvings on the roof bosses show sheep heads, the source of the wealth which allowed this church to be built. Rings in the wall were used to tether horses, so the floor must have once been lower. In the church entrance is a sign telling people to remove their pattens – wooden overshoes. St Andrew's has a memorial to its 19th century Greek vicar, while at Terrington a Table of Kindred and Affinity tells you which of your relatives not to marry – a vital point in an isolated community! Claude Coates, local fruit grower and benefactor, is commemorated by a modern plate glass window at Walsoken. Terrington St Clement has a plate glass window commemorating local men who died in the First World War, while West Walton has a 17th century board recalling more flooding, plus a statue of St Mary by Norfolk wood sculptor Anton Wagner. The rather spartan interiors of most English churches date from the iconoclasm (breaking of sacred images) of the 16th and 17th centuries, particularly during the civil wars. Plate glass, colourful paintings and statuary largely disappeared in this era. At Terrington St Clement, though, in 1887 two statues of saints were discovered, having been hidden for three centuries. The 1544 font at Walsoken is a rare survivor, showing the seven Catholic sacraments and the crucifixion. The Diocese of Ely has produced a well illustrated Church Trail information pack encouraging the faithful – and students of history and architecture – to visit these churches. Entitled Marshland Majesty, it is one of a series promoting others in the fens. These churches have been vulnerable to theft, so visitors need to check opening arrangements.

The Italian job

In 1394 the city state of Florence buried a great warlord, the saviour of its independence. However, this was no Italian or continental exponent of Renaissance warfare, but a man of obscure origins born in the Colne Valley, Essex, 74 years earlier.

The only way is Essex?

If he said so, you had better believe it. Sir John Hawkwood was not a man to argue with lightly. His life story is one of extremes and contradictions. Born and raised in an East Anglian village, he went on to walk with princes and popes, a soldier of great talent who combined chivalry with brutality typical of his age. Leaving England at a young age he carved out a career as a mercenary, but is remembered with honour in his north Essex home village. According to Florentine historians, John Hawkwood was born in about 1320 in Sible Hedingham, just south of the Suffolk border. His father was Gilbert, a well-to-do tanner and landowner. His family were "well born although not of grand lineage". John was the second of three sons, the eldest of whom was also named John. On their father's death in 1340, as was traditional in English families, the eldest inherited the land, the youngest went into the Church and John, the middle son, was left to forge his own career. A later English legend insists he served an apprenticeship with a London tailor, but this seems to contradict his family's social position. Another version maintains he was press-ganged into the army. Although both these stories are not to be dismissed, it seems more likely he chose to become a soldier. The timing could not have been better. King Edward III was at war with the French, and needed all the men he could raise. Hawkwood is said to have begun his military career in about 1343 under the command of John de Vere, Earl of Oxford, and fought at the battles of Crecy and Poitiers, though evidence is lacking for his presence at these events. Some say Hawkwood was knighted by Edward the Black Prince, son of

Edward III. These were great victories for the English, particularly due to the longbow. Fame and fortune followed – for some. But when peace eventually broke out, and the kings and nobles counted their lands, honours and booty, the common soldiers had to fend for themselves. Many formed themselves into self-employed companies, living off the French countryside and terrorising the unfortunate inhabitants. They were the original freelances. Hawkwood's service to the English crown ended with the Treaty of Bretigny in 1360. Moving to Burgundy he joined one of the free companies, later fighting against the pope's army near Avignon. Three years later he commanded the most famous of them all, the White Company.

Heroes or villains?

It depends on your point of view. Arthur Conan Doyle, in his 1891 book The White Company based loosely on Hawkwood's career, portrayed the English soldiers as chivalrous knights. But the truth was the brutal freebooting companies devastated lands and people. Contemporary French chronicler Jean de Froissart bitterly maintained they chose "the worst among them" as leaders. Certainly these were harsh times, and the soldiers lived by their own rules and code of conduct. Like modern soldiers of fortune they gave their loyalty to the highest bidder and did not hesitate to change sides. The 14th century was a particularly lucrative time for business. As opportunities became scarcer in France, avaricious eyes turned south. To Italy. The Renaissance era affected Italy before northern Europe. Improved learning created great wealth, artistic sophistication and luxury. It also forged political instability. Italy was a patchwork of independent city states. All warred with each other. Concentrating on trade, they hired international troops to fight for them, and paid top wages. It was a mercenary's dream come true. Hawkwood first crossed the Alps in 1363, when the Marquis of Montferrato hired his White Company to fight against Milan. Aware that Italy offered rich pickings Hawkwood and his men stayed there. Whatever his personal morality, professionally he changed sides when it suited him. The White

Company fought for Pisa against Florence, then Perugia against the papacy. In 1370 he fought against his former employers, Pisa and the Florentines, who were now their allies. Eventually he and his company joined the pope's forces. His reputation as a *condottiero* – the Italian term for a mercenary – grew. They knew him as *Giovanni Acuto*, "John the Sharp", and he was reckoned as less savage than his competitors (though they did set the bar rather high). He may have taken the view that war was nothing personal, just business. More often than not, he was victorious, the elite performer of the mercenary world. He was said to be illiterate, his contracts being read to him and signed on his behalf. Hawkwood played employers against each other, accepting a contract then demanding payment from opponents in order not to attack them – or sometimes just keeping the money.

Good business?

Hawkwood thrived. He bought estates in Romagna and Tuscany, married the Donnina Visconti, daughter of the duke of Milan, and was later ambassador to the Roman court for English king Richard II. In 1377 he fell out with the papacy after he masterminded the destruction of the town of Cesena. The story goes that he wanted to spare the townsfolk's lives, but a cardinal had them massacred. Now he fought against the papacy, and this led him into the service of wealthy Florence. That city's greatest enemy was Milan, and the two went to war in the 1390s. Hawkwood, now 70 years old, led Florence's army with such distinction the Florentines credited him with saving them from destruction. They granted him citizenship and a pension. He died in March, 1394, and was buried in the Duomo (cathedral).

Hawkwood's conduct was not frowned upon. Modern concepts of nationalism and patriotism were not as fixed as they are now, so changing sides was not out of the ordinary. Richard II requested his body be returned to England, and his children settled in Essex. In Sible Hedingham church there is a Hawkwood memorial chapel. If you brave the queues, and visit Florence's magnificent Duomo, look out for the memorial fresco created in his honour in 1436 by Paolo Uccello.

The fighting Heydons

There never was a Paston poor, nor a Heydon a coward

This old Norfolk proverb reflects the fortunes of two of the county's prominent feuding families.

Pastons used the pen. . . presumably the Heydons favoured the sword! Generations of historians and readers have benefited from the surviving correspondence left behind by north Norfolk's Paston family. Originally of peasant stock, they rose through law and the land, with a bit of military muscle thrown in, during the 15th and 16th centuries. The Heydons were their contemporaries, and the two clans were at one time mortal foes before burying the hatchet. While the Pastons turned out to be a fairly pragmatic lot, the Heydons had a self-destructive streak. Later members of the family were fighters, duellists, astrologers and mathematicians. They picked fights with monarchs, Parliament, their neighbours – and each other to the extent that they have entered Norfolk legend for their belligerence and eccentricity.

Normal for Norfolk?

The family came from the village of Heydon, and they worked the land as peasant farmers. Their surname was originally Baxter, meaning Baker, but they later changed it to the far grander sounding Heydon. The founder of the Paston line, Clement, followed a similar route. In the aftermath of the Black Death of 1348-9, which killed up to half the population, enterprising peasants took advantage of the shortage of labour to free themselves – and make their descendants rich. Key to this was owning land, and possessing the legal means to keep hold of it. So John Heydon was trained in the law. Tough, cunning and occasionally ruthless, he was prepared to use harsh measures to aggrandise the family estates. At Baconsthorpe, near Holt, he built a palatial fortified home. It was a castle, but also a statement of the family's wealth. Begun in the 1480s, it was by the standards of the time luxury accommodation. Built of knapped flint, it boasted state-of-the-art firing slots for early cannon, a moat and drawbridge. A home for a man who expected trouble, but also wanted some style. Although he thrived in business, his personal life was a mess. When his wife Eleanor had a child by another man, he threatened to cut off her nose and kill the baby.

Not a man to cross!

The Pastons were building their own property empire nearby, so it was inevitable the two should clash. At one time, Margaret Paston and her outnumbered retainers were expelled from a manor house at Gresham by an armed mob "by the excitation and procuring of John Heydon". In the 1440s and 1450s Judge John Heydon was involved in disputes between the citizens of Norwich and its priory. Facing a court case, Heydon gathered 60 armed men and rode into Norwich trying to incite the citizens to an uprising. Disputes rumbled on for decades. It was a time of unrest in England, with central government crumbling. The series of conflicts now known as the Wars of the Roses caused chaos, and the Pastons and Heydons were on different sides. Not quite Capulet and Montague though; John's death in 1478, probably from plague, ended the feud. The marriage of Bridget Heydon and William Paston a decade later consigned it to history.

Everyone happy. . .

The 16th century was a time of plenty for Norfolk's gentry. Baconsthorpe boomed, with the family presiding over an economy enriched by sheep farming. But the Heydons' self-destructive streak and ability to choose the wrong side came to the fore. Sir Christopher Heydon (born 1561) was a soldier, MP – and astrologer. His first major battle was with his parents. A lengthy dispute over his Baconsthorpe inheritance, in which his father spitefully threatened to demolish the castle, only ended with the intervention of Queen Elizabeth I. It saddled him with £14,000 debts – a mind-boggling sum then. Next the family took up duelling. Christopher's proposed duel with Sir John Townshend was prevented by the Privy Council, but a later fight in Norwich between younger brother John and political rival Sir Robert Mansell ended with John's hand being severed. More trouble followed. Heydon had been at Cambridge with the Earl of Essex, later the queen's favourite. He was a good patron and friend, and Christopher fought alongside the earl in an attack on Cadiz in 1596 (for which he was knighted). Friendship was one thing, but when hot-headed Essex rebelled against the queen in 1601 it might have been wiser to have walked away. But Christopher and his brother led troops through the streets of London. The revolt collapsed instantly, and Essex was executed. Heydon's friendship with chief minister Sir Robert Cecil saved his life, but his public career was over – and he had to pay a £2,000 fine for his part in the rebellion. With a total of 14 children, a younger brother on the run in exile in the Netherlands, and Baconsthorpe mortaged to the hilt, Heydon consoled himself by publishing widely on the subject of astrology.

Time to play it safe?

The Heydon courage didn't allow for compromise. Sir Christopher's sons William and John were both soldiers. William, the eldest, was drowned in an expedition to France in 1627. John forged a military career, commanding King Charles' artillery at the Battle of Edgefield in 1642. He was the king's head of ordnance at Oxford throughout the war, in charge of supplying Royalist armies. Parliament confiscated his lands. Although he later bought them back, his once splendid family castle was crumbling. Heydon had to sell off a lot of the stone to pay his debts, much of which went to build Felbrigg Hall, near Cromer. As the family fortunes fell into terminal disrepair, so did Baconsthorpe. A London merchant bought the castle, and later a doctor named Zurishaddair Lang lived there. The gatehouse was inhabited until gales brought it down in 1921. Ruined Baconsthorpe sits in a quiet country spot three miles east of Holt, its gatehouse hinting at the splendour of the fighting Heydons. They live on in folklore and local legend.

Where angels soar

It is a church that really is on the side of the angels. St Wendreda's in March can trace its history from an Anglo-Saxon princess through to an Australian war hero.

From Sir John Betjeman to murder mystery author Dorothy L Sayers, it is looking up that has inspired visitors to the church, on the outskirts of the Cambridgeshire fenland town. Its double hammerbeam angel roof got Poet Laureate Betjeman so fired up he declared he would "cycle 40 miles in a head wind" to see it. Take a trip to March, and you'll see what all the fuss was about. The story goes back to the life of the eighth century Saint Wendreda, after whom the church is named, and whose medieval cult inspired the glories of the present building.

Who was Saint Wendreda?

Said to be the daughter of East Anglian King Aenna, she came from a family with impeccable Christian credentials. At a time when the new religion was putting down roots among the Anglo-Saxon people of England, Wendreda and her fellow royal sisters Etheldreda, founder of the monastery at Ely, and Sexburga became enthusiastic missionaries spreading the new religion. Shunning the life of a princess, Wendreda dedicated herself to healing. Eventually she settled in the small settlement called Mercheford, then populated by humble fishermen by the River Nene. After her death she was buried at the since renamed March, and a shrine grew up around the tomb. Pilgrims visited the isolated spot, mostly having to travel by boat to this island in the then undrained fenland.

Presumably that was the first church

No trace of the Saxon church remains, and the chances are it was a fairly rudimentary wooden building. The Normans, as was their habit, built the first stone construction in the later 11th century. Stone being scarce in the fens, it had to be transported by water from the great quarry at Barnack, near Stamford. The font is said to be the oldest in Cambridgeshire, dating from those early Norman days, although it was later modified. No doubt early pilgrims were moved to visit the saint's resting place, but by this time her body was on the move. In the early 11th century, with the rampaging Danes closing in, the desperate Anglo-Saxon army dug up Wendreda's bones hoping they would bring them fortune. Sadly, this did not work, and they were beaten at the Battle of Ashingdon in 1016. But even this added to the lustre of Wendreda's legend. Conquering Danish king Canute seized her relics, and was soon converted to Christianity – partially inspired by the saint, according to the monks. Her remains continued their journey, resting at Canterbury for the next 300 years. But in 1343 she returned to March, enshrined in the church dedicated to her memory. Wendreda's return sparked the church's golden era. The church was restored, and pilgrims resumed their visits, among them the sick in search of a cure. More rebuilding went on after the Black Death, much of it paid for by local trade guilds, which had an important religious function. Wealthy local patrons included Antony Hansart and his wife, who were commemorated in a 16th century brass still in the church.

What about that roof?
Plaudits have rained in for this glorious piece of art – but it has had to survive two deadly enemies; man and beetles. Carved in English oak, the roof depicts 120 angel figures projected from the hammerbeams and fixed to the king-post trusses. Other figures include apostles, saints and martyrs and other angels holding medieval musical instruments. Held to represent the "summit of the woodcarver's art" the roof was constructed from 1523 to 1526 by Suffolk craftsmen, the wood carried to March by water. The date is significant; in 1526 Cardinal Thomas Wolsey issued an Indulgence to the town of March allowing them a new priest; within a few years the turmoil of the Reformation was under way and the old Church and its artistry were swept away. King Henry VIII's Commissioners arrived in March in 1546 at a time when

saints' relics and extravagent religious icons were being done away with across England, as they were regarded by Protestant reformers as Catholic superstition. But the townspeople were in no mood to lose their wonderful angel roof. According to local legend, they wined and dined the Commissioners, who shut down the trade guilds and went away with a lot of church silver for the king's bulging coffers – but left the roof alone. As for Saint Wendreda's relics, they disappeared, never to be seen again. Perhaps some of her diehard adherents buried her bones to save them, and the secret died with them; it is likely we will never know.

What about the beetles?
Death watch beetle gnawed away at the roof and did a lot of damage. It cost several thousand pounds and some resplicing to remedy it. During the early 1980s the roof started leaking, and the lead had to be recast. It costs a lot to maintain such an old building. Today visitors are impressed by the deceptively spacious interior and the light that floods in. A fine stained glass window depicts Wendreda and another East Anglian saint, Edmund the Martyr. Author Dorothy L Sayers, whose father was vicar at nearby Christchurch, was inspired by the roof to give it a mention in her Lord Peter Wimsey tale, The Nine Taylors.

And the Australian war hero?
In July, 1944, 21-year-old Pilot Officer Jim Hocking, of the Royal Australian Air Force, was commanding a Short Stirling bomber. Fire broke out, and the engines died. Courageous Hocking ordered his crew to bale out and, to avoid crashing onto the town of March, guided it to crash land in a field beyond St Wendreda's. He was killed as the aircraft burst into flames, but many civilian lives were no doubt saved by his self-sacrifice. More than 40 years later in 1988, following an investigation by local newspaper the Cambridgeshire Times, a memorial honouring Hocking's selfless act was unveiled in the church. Today, the famous roof is considered one of the finest of its kind, and among very few surviving in East Anglia.

Tudors

and

Stuarts

The tombs of Katherine Willoughby, Duchess of Suffolk, and her second husband can be found in St James's Church, Spilsby, where her family chapel is situated. She lived an eventful life under four Tudor monarchs.

Great fire of Norwich

"All life is brief, and frail all man's estate. City, farewell: I mourn thy cruel fate."
In 1507 the poet John Skelton (1460–1529) wrote of two destructive fires in his Lament for the City of Norwich.

Medieval and early modern cities were particularly vulnerable to destructive fires. Norwich endured a series of conflagrations in the early years of the 16th century that left it scarred for decades. The heart of the city was ripped out, with more than 700 houses being destroyed. Following earlier fires in 1467 and 1505, there were two disasters within a month of one another in 1507. First, on April 25, a fire broke out near an inn called the Popinjay in Tombland, near the cathedral. With thatched roofs quickly catching the flames, it spread towards St Andrew's and the Franciscan monastery there, and into several parishes, stretching as far as Pottergate. It must have been an intense blaze, as it crossed the river into St George's Colegate. It took four terrible days for the fire to burn itself out. As if that was not bad enough, on June 4 a fresh fire broke out. Contemporary accounts relate it began in the Colegate house of a French surgeon, whose (presumably anglicised) name was Peter Johnson.

How did the fires start – and why were they so destructive?
A modern health and safety expert would have closed down 16th century Norwich, and most other towns as an accident waiting to happen. Buildings were largely timber-built, they had wooden chimneys and roofs made of thatch. It was a recipe for disaster. Some of these were natural; in 1463 lightning set the wooden spire of the cathedral on fire, but most were manmade. Buildings went up largely unregulated, the crowded living conditions exacerbated by lack of space within the confining city walls. People were ill-equipped to deal with fires, there being no trained firefighters. Lacking safety matches

---

people might fetch a bucket of burning coals from a neighbour rather than waste time getting a light from a tinder-box. Households were reliant on candles for light, an obvious fire risk. "Fear candle, good wife," wrote the agriculturalist and poet Thomas Tusser, who lived in Norfolk later in the century. "Fear candle in hay loft, in barn and shed." All these places were at risk, when a moment of carelessness, or an unlucky draught, could knock them over. Workplaces were more often than not based in people's homes. Industrial practices did not help; dyers, brewers, blacksmiths and soapboilers, among others, worked with fire, and safety measures were rudimentary. Once a fire took hold, it was hard to stop. It was all hands to the job, but a few leather buckets, ladders and hooks for pulling down burning thatch were about as far as the technology went.

What was the damage in Norwich?
Modern estimates reckon up to 40 per cent of the city's houses were burnt down. Modern excavations in Pottergate in 1973 showed properties had been burnt to the ground, leaving only their cellars – or undercrofts. In Elm Hill, close to Tombland, apparently only one building survived. The beguinage (house for religious women), now the Britons Arms cafe, alone stood undamaged by the time the smoke had died away. It only survived as it was one of the few buildings made of stone. In Tombland itself one of the few surviving buildings was the ancient construction, now once again the Louis Marchesi pub, itself with an impressive undercroft in use to this day. "England's chief ornament in ashes lies; O city, what of thee can now be said," declared Diss poet and clergyman John Skelton in his lament for Norwich. The aftermath of the fires temporarily devastated the city's economy. Properties that normally brought in £5 rent to the cathedral's coffers only yielded 33s in 1505, and just 19s 4d two years later, according to the almoner's account. The human cost was heavy too. With no such thing as insurance, a family who had been well off with a business and property one day was reduced to dire poverty the next. They had to rely on charity from church and neighbours. With so many homeless

the distress was acute, and many would have despaired. A group of city aldermen was sent to address the privy council in London to raise some funds for reconstruction; that tight-fisted Tudor monarch Henry VII was having none of it. It is a tribute to the wealth and determination of the citizens that the city rose from the ashes so quickly. Picturesque Elm Hill, in particular, bears testament to the rapid rebuilding. Many of the houses there today date from the mid-1500s, and give a good indication of how our Tudor ancestors lived. Some have medieval undercrofts, reminders of the Norwich that was burnt to the ground.

Wasn't it time to take some fire precautions?

The city decreed that all houses built after 1507 should have roofs built of slate and tile. Easier said than done. Sixty years later the city council blamed the abundance of thatched roofs for "diverse casualties and mischances", and bemoaned a lack of buckets and ladders to fight blazes. Fire remained a hazard, not just in Norwich. The town of Wymondham was the scene of a terrible blaze in 1615, this time the result of arson, and more than 300 people lost property. In Beccles in 1586 a fire that began when some genius fired a gun up a chimney in order to clean it claimed 80 houses. It was clear the lessons learnt in Norwich had not been heeded everywhere. It was not until the end of the 18th century that Thomas Bignold founded Norwich Union, providing fire insurance for householders. In common with other such companies, the Union had its own fire service, and would extinguish blazes at houses which bore a plate confirming they paid their premiums.

No such problems now!

Fires can still wreak havoc. Nobody in the city can forget the two fires that destroyed a pair of Norwich landmarks in the mid-1990s – the main city library and the historic 18th century Assembly House. Both were spectacularly and successfully rebuilt, much as the Norwich of 1507 rose again.

'Bishy Barnabee'

"This cannibal in three years' space three hundred martyrs slew. They were his food, he loved so blood, he spared none he knew."
Foxe's Book of Martyrs
(Acts and Monuments), 1563

Well, he sounds like a bloodthirsty villain. . .

This bloodcurdling quote needs to be put into context. It is taken from one of the most influential works of literature in British history – John Foxe's Book of Martyrs. It's a damning verdict, but does it tell the real story of Bishop Edmund Bonner? This clergyman, former rector of East Dereham's St Nicholas' Church, where his former house is now a museum, has had a spectacularly bad press. He has gone down in folklore as the henchman of 'Bloody Mary', who burnt Protestant martyrs with relish. In Norfolk it is believed his name is forever linked to one of our best-known insects. It is difficult to separate truth from propaganda and 'fake news', particularly where the bitter religious conflict of the English Reformation is concerned.

It was certainly an age of intolerance

At a time when religion was central to everyone's existence, it was a serious matter. England, like much of Europe, was riven by religious dissent in the 16th century. It only narrowly avoided the kind of devastating civil war and massacres that occurred in France and Germany. For ordinary people, it must have been a worrying era; what was accepted practice one day became heresy the next. With King Henry VIII breaking with Rome's authority in the 1530s, his son Edward's Protestant reforms in the 1540s, followed by Mary's about-turn back to Catholicism in the 1550s, it was hard to know which way to turn. As so often throughout history, small groups of influential and articulate fanatics were able to impose their views on the population as a whole.

Presumably, Bonner fell into that category. . .

Religious conservative is probably the best description. Born in Worcestershire in about 1500, he studied law at Oxford and entered Cardinal Wolsey's civil service after being ordained as a priest. Bonner stayed loyal to Wolsey when the Cardinal fell in 1529, but he had already proved his worth to Thomas Cromwell, the king's new go-to man. Bonner became Henry's ambassador to Rome. He was sent to try to persuade Pope Clement VII to grant Henry a divorce from Katharine of Aragon. Like Wolsey before him, he failed. . . but by now it was a hopeless task. Bonner's reputation was untarnished; he was rewarded with the rector's living at Dereham, which he took up from 1534-40 until appointed Bishop of London. He was also ambassador to the Holy Roman Emperor, Charles V, in Spain and Germany. In England, Henry VIII's iron hand kept the lid on the pace of religious change. Reformers were kept in check by fear of the king's retribution. Everything changed after he died in 1547. For Edmund Bonner it was a turning point. Up until this point he had been able to go along with royal policy; the Protestant reforms put into action by the government of the boy king Edward VI were too much for him to stomach. New prayer books, married priests and the destruction of church ornaments were a bridge too far for many conservatives. Bonner persistently resisted the changes, and was imprisoned in London's Marshalsea Prison. If it was not for young Edward's early death after six years on the throne, Bonner may have been locked up indefinitely. As it was, the king's sister Mary became queen in July, 1553. She saw it as her sacred duty to return England to what she believed was the true faith. Within days Bonner was released and restored to his bishopric. Now he was the spearhead of the assault on Protestantism, "looking into the windows of men's souls" as a later monarch put it. Following her marriage to Philip of Spain, Queen Mary turned the heat on heretics – literally. Bonner's job, as Bishop of London, was to question suspects, beat them down and get a confession, hopefully persuading them of the error of their ways. Some described him as a rough, coarse, hot-tempered, red-faced fellow; others said he was honest, courteous and gentlemanly. Maybe it depended on which side of the interrogation you were on. There is no denying the end result. If he did not turn the rack himself, he was certainly complicit in the legal torture that followed.

Not to mention the burnings. . .

Public burnings of heretics took place on market days to attract the largest possible audience. Men, women and even some children died terrible deaths. If the executioners were merciful they would pile the fires up high and the victim was more likely to die quickly of carbon monoxide poisoning before the flames got to them. Often though, they were ordered to make it a slow, agonising job. In all, about 270 people were executed within the space of three years from 1555 to 1558. Was Bonner ultimately responsible? Records show he was not the ogre he was later painted by Foxe. He tried to save people's lives by getting them to recant their views. There is a letter on record from Mary and Philip ordering the bishop to hurry up and get rid of even more heretics. Perhaps he feared he'd be next up at the stake if he failed in his duty. Bonner showed no mercy to his former boss. Archbishop of Canterbury Thomas Cranmer and the respected reformers Nicholas Ridley and Hugh Latimer were condemned to burn. This celebrated trio died bravely; Cranmer had signed a document repudiating Protestantism but, at the last minute, had a change of heart and thrust his hand that had held the pen into the flames. Latimer's final reported words were legendary: "Be of good comfort, Master Ridley, we shall this day light such a candle in England as I trust shall never be put out." Of the Protestants executed during Queen Mary's reign, most came from southern England. East Anglia – Essex, Suffolk, Cambridgeshire and Norfolk – were particularly affected. Dozens were put to death in Colchester, for example. They included clergyman John Lawrence, executed in March, 1555. Others were burnt at Maldon, Braintree, Rayleigh, Stratford and Saffron Walden. Two vicars of Hadleigh, Suffolk, were burnt; Rowland Taylor early in 1555 and Sir Richard Yeoman at Norwich three years later. People from all walks of life were involved. Essex men Stephen Knight, William Pygot and Nicholas Chamberlain worked as a barber, butcher and weaver respectively. Both Ipswich and Ely had a rash of martyrs. Agnes Potten and Joan Truchfield were among the few women put to death, at Ipswich's Cornhill in February, 1556, while Upwell village constable William Wolsey was among several who died on Cathedral Green, Ely. Bury St Edmunds was another centre for execution, Mendlesham weaver Robert Lawson and Thomas Spurdance, described as a "servant of the queen", were put to death there. In Norwich weaver's wife Cecily Ormes and pewterer's spouse Elizabeth Cooper died at Lollards Pit, where heretics had been burnt for many years. They perished at the same spot as glover Thomas Hudson, husbandman William Seaman and Wymondham's Richard Crashfield. Thetford, Beccles, Walsingham and Yoxford also saw judicial killings for heresy.

Did this turn people against Bishop Bonner?
Many in London hated him, but then the capital and south-east were becoming inclined towards Protestantism. When Mary died in 1558, and Queen Elizabeth I came to the throne, his days were numbered. At her accession she snubbed him and when her government banned the Mass he defied the law. "I possess three things, soul, body and property," he declared. "Of the two latter you can dispose at your pleasure, but as to the soul, God alone can command me." His old cell at the Marshalsea once again became his familiar haunt for the final decade of his life. He died in 1569. Under Elizabeth I it was the Catholics' turn to be persecuted. Foxe's Martyrs, for many years as familiar to English readers as the Bible, told the tale from the now ruling Protestant side. It sealed Bonner's reputation as a bogeyman.

What about this insect?
In Norfolk the ladybird is known as the Bishy Barnabee. Some say this refers to the red flames that consumed Bonner's victims. His former home in St Withburga Lane, Dereham, is now the Bishop Bonner's Cottage Museum.

Suffolk's daring duchess

She could have been Henry VIII's seventh wife. She may even have been Queen of Poland. She did become Duchess of Suffolk as a teenage bride. Catherine Willoughby led a fascinating life. A committed Protestant, she lived at a time of peril and conflict.

A high flyer of the Tudor court

Catherine Willoughby was born in 1519 at Parham Old Hall, near Framlingham in Suffolk. Her parents were as well connected as you could hope to be; father William Lord Willoughby de Eresby held more manors than was strictly necessary in Suffolk, Norfolk and Lincolnshire, while her mother was Spanish – Maria de Salinas, lady-in-waiting, friend and confidante of Queen Katharine of Aragon. Born with a silver spoon she may have been, but the young Catherine (probably named in honour of the Queen, her godmother) was to have no easy childhood. When she was a mere seven years old, her father died. As her infant brother had also passed on, Catherine was left as only child and her father's sole heiress. That was not as enviable a position as it sounds. As a child and a female, she was vulnerable to every avaricious relative of the family with a claim to make. Soon the vultures were circling, keen to acquire land and titles. Catherine's inheritance was disputed in the courts for many years to come. She was quickly made a ward of King Henry VIII, who passed on this valuable wardship to his brother-in-law.

Another prestigious connection. . .

Charles Brandon was the glamour boy of the glittering Tudor court in the early years of Henry's reign. The young king's jousting partner, he had almost blotted his copybook when he married Henry's much-loved younger sister without asking permission. Mary Tudor had briefly been Queen of France, but her much older husband died. The king quickly got over his annoyance at Brandon's cheek – and raised

Katherine Willoughby became Duchess of Suffolk when she married Henry VIII's jousting partner, Charles Brandon. She is remembered by this memorial, in the magnificent Willoughby family chapel, to be seen at St James's Church, Spilsby, in Lincolnshire. Inset, above, Hans Holbein's miniature portrait of the duchess as a young woman.

Left, a carving of a mermaid in Upper Sheringham Church. The village is the site of a well-known mermaid legend.

A statue representing Tiw, the god of war, can be seen in the gardens at Anglesey Abbey, near Cambridge. Tiw gives his name to our modern Tuesday, one of the mythological origins for our days of the week.

Blakeney St Nicholas's Church seen from the coast path. Now well inland, Blakeney was once a major port on the north Norfolk coast.

City of dragons. After the cult of Saint George was suppressed during the Reformation, Norwich ditched the saint, but kept the dragon. Above, a dragon features on the top of the Ethelbert Gate to Norwich Cathedral. Left, the Go-Go Dragons were a popular feature in the summer of 2015. Here, one is seen in Cathedral Close with a statue of another Norfolk icon, Horatio Nelson.

Right, return of the saints. Part of the restored rood screen at St Helen's Church, Ranworth, one of the few surviving intact in East Anglia.

There are many legends about the statues known as Samson and Hercules. These replicas stand guard outside a restaurant on Norwich's Tombland. Their colour scheme has changed over the years, but they are a familiar landmark.

People have been downing pints of ale at the Adam and Eve pub in Norwich, since at least 1249. It may well be the oldest pub in the city. Unless, of course, you know better. . .

Medieval hard man Sir John Hawkwood was born in Essex, but his mercenary career saw him fight with huge success in France and Italy. He is honoured with this inscription in Florence's Duomo.

Below, Peter the Wild Man made a brief visit to Norfolk in 1751.

The Wild Man

The Wild Man pub is thought to commemorate Peter the Wild Boy (c.1711-1785), a feral child found in the forests of Hanover in about 1725, who was, for a time, kept by King George I as a curiosity. In 1751 he mysteriously turned up in Norwich and was briefly imprisoned in the Bridewell as a vagrant before being returned to his guardians in Berkhampsted in Hertfordshire.

Nine days' wonder. Elizabethan funny man Will Kemp made waves when he danced all the way from London to Norwich. This wood sculpture in Chapelfield Gardens marks his feat. If only he'd got on better with Shakespeare. . .

Explorer Matthew Flinders performed great feats of navigation around Australia. On the left is a statue of him and his cat Trim in his native Donington. Above, a stained glass window in the church there recalls his exploits and those of other explorers.

Left, Archbishop Stigand (or Stigant) was born in Norwich, and went on to have a long career in the Anglo-Saxon royal court. His luck ran out after the Norman Conquest of 1066.

Last stand. The Britons Arms was the only building in Elm Hill to survive the great fire of Norwich in 1507, which caused huge devastation in a city of wooden buildings. Today it is a cafe in a popular tourist area.

When Baconsthorpe Castle was first built, it declared that the mighty Heydon family were the dominant force in this part of Norfolk, near Holt. Today, it is a ruin at the end of a quiet country lane.

Coke of Norfolk is honoured in this relief to be found in the grounds of Holkham Hall. Back in 1842 he was given a grand send-off at his funeral.

On the side of the angels. The decorated hammerbeam roof at St Wendreda's Church, March, has impressed visitors since the early 1500s.

him to be Duke of Suffolk. He was Henry's favourite fighting man, heroic if not the most astute commander. By the early 1530s a little of the shine was fading, as he aged. His duchess died in 1533, by which he had betrothed his son Henry to his ward, the teenage Catherine.

All in the family. . .
Except that young Henry didn't marry the heiress. His father, the Duke, did just six weeks after his wife died. Possibly, he feared losing her lands. Also, his son was only 10 years old, and he died shortly afterwards, another victim of the high child mortality of the era. Quite what the 14-year-old bride thought of being married to her 49-year-old guardian has gone unrecorded. Even at the time it raised an eyebrow or two. Eustace de Chapuys, ambassador of the Holy Roman Emperor, remarked on the "novelty" of the marriage. The Duke of Suffolk had been sent into Lincolnshire and the North to put down the Pilgrimage of Grace in 1536, and he stayed in the area to keep an eye on things. The couple divided their time between the court in London and estates in Lincolnshire. These included their main residence at Grimsthorpe, near Bourne, and Tattershall Castle. Despite the age gap, they had two sons, Henry and Charles, born in 1535 and 1537 respectively. The Suffolks were regulars at court, officially welcoming the king's fourth wife, Anne of Cleves, in 1540. The marriage ended in 1545, when the duke died. It left the duchess an attractive widow, wealthy, in her mid-twenties and highly eligible. Some said the king himself was interested.

Out of the frying pan. . .?
Henry was married to his sixth wife, the duchess's best friend, Catherine Parr. Who knows what was going through the old tyrant's mind? For the Duchess of Suffolk it may well have been a relief when he died early in 1547. Narrow escape, perhaps? Catherine Willoughby had a mind of her own. Well educated, known for her wit and good humour, she was outspoken. Like Queen Catherine Parr, she was a Protestant. In Lincolnshire she promoted reforming clergy and teachers. She funded Protestant literature, helping the queen publish

Lamentation of a Sinner, a controversial reforming theological work, and supported leading Protestant publisher John Day, who later printed the first edition of Foxe's Martyrs. Bishop Stephen Gardner was the leading conservative cleric of the day, and the duchess disliked him. She named her pet spaniel 'Gardner', so she could amuse herself and fellow courtiers by ordering the dog to come to heel. For all that, she was a woman in a man's world, and lived in dangerous times. On one occasion she offended chief minister Lord Burghley, and had to make a formal apology "on her knees", while cleric Hugh Latimer, her Protestant ally, warned her that "women should keep their tongues in better order".

What about her personal life?

Some reports say she turned down a marriage proposal from King Sigismund of Poland, of whom more later. Instead, in direct contrast to her first, arranged marriage, she wed a second time for love. Richard Bertie was an officer in her own household, her Master of Horse, when they married. Like her, he was a convinced Protestant. Tragically, both her sons from her first marriage had earlier died of fever while students at university. Soon though a new family of children were on the way, their daughter being born in 1553. By that time Queen Mary was on the throne. The couple were known as Protestants, and were at risk of prosecution. They fled into exile for their own safety. According to John Foxe, author of Foxe's Martyrs, they eluded Mary's agents, making it to safety in Germany. From there they called on the protection of King Sigismund. The Polish monarch had clearly got over Catherine's refusal to marry him; he granted her and her husband asylum in Lithuania, then ruled by Poland. This period of exile ended when Elizabeth I became queen. Protestants began to return to England, the duchess and her family among them. They settled at Grimsthorpe, where Catherine died in 1580, aged 61. Her husband lived just two years longer. The Duchess of Suffolk was buried at St James's Church, Spilsby, near to many of her ancestors. Her resting place is marked by a fine memorial.

Robert Kett's Rebellion

In 1949 a plaque was put up at Norwich castle. It commemorated the 500th anniversary of the death of "a notable leader in the long struggle of the common people of England to escape from a servile life into freedom of just conditions". That man was Robert Kett – but was his uprising as straightforward as the inscription suggests?

Who was Robert Kett?

He was a prosperous merchant tanner and landowner from Wymondham. A respectable man in his town, prominent in the local trade guilds. How did he end up leading a huge army of rebels who seized Norwich and were only crushed, at great loss of life, by a large mercenary army? Norfolk's upheavals in the summer of 1549 were not isolated; much of the country was in uproar. Following the death of Henry VIII, his son, the young King Edward VI was too young to govern. A council headed by Protector Somerset – Edward's uncle – held power and instituted widespread Protestant reform. This ignited conservative rebellion in the West Country. East Anglia was not immune to religious dissent, but economic and social strife tipped Norfolk into rebellion.

Why?

Wealthy gentry landowners were enclosing common land for private use. This hurt the 'poor commons', the working people who lost pasture and timber rights. This affected people in both the city of Norwich and the countryside. Many resented the gentry who had enriched themselves in the Reformation, feeling that the balance of society was being tipped. By June, 1549, it seemed the government of the popular Somerset – the 'Good Duke' – was moving against enclosures. Whether encouraged by this, or acting independently, commoners from Attleborough began breaking up fences and reclaiming land used by the community for generations. One landowner targeted was Robert Kett. In early July he agreed to lead the commoners to march on Norwich and "subdue the power of great men". Kett's motives have long been argued over; to what extent did he control the rebels he led, and what was he trying to achieve? Events spiralled, and he was at the head of thousands of angry men.

Meanwhile, in Norwich. . .

The reaction of the city authorities was ambiguous. Perhaps the mayor, Thomas Codd, and his aldermen knew Kett had sympathisers in the poorer areas of the city. The north and south parishes of the city were poor, crowded and seething with discontent. When trouble broke out, the rebels had allies within the walls. Codd met Kett's men – estimated at up to 16,000, though that may be an exaggeration – at Eaton Wood, and refused them entry to Norwich. The rebels skirted to the east, and set up camp on Mousehold Heath. Things moved rapidly; hostages were taken and housed both in the castle and in Surrey Place overlooking the city. There, at the top of what is now known as Kett's Hill, Robert set up his headquarters. He administered a form of justice from beneath the 'Oak of Reformation'. All seemed orderly, and negotiations began, following a familiar pattern in previous peasant risings which had ended without bloodshed.

What was the official reaction?

The rebels issued a list of complaints to Somerset's representatives, demanding land and education reform. Rebels stormed the city in mid-July, overcoming weak resistance. Things could have ended peacefully, but the arrival of a 1,500-strong royal army under the Marquis of Northampton changed everything. On August 1, a diversion took Northampton to the Pockthorpe gate. The rebels stormed across the Bishop Bridge, which stands to this day. In a series of running battles, the ineffective Northampton's second-in-command Lord Sheffield was knocked off his horse and killed. Defeated, the royal troops retreated. The rebels ruled in Norwich. For now. But the writing was on the wall. In late August the Earl of Warwick reached Norwich. Unfortunately for the rebels, this warrior knew his business. Accompanied by a force 8,000 to 12,000 strong, a mix of elite Swiss and German mercenaries ('landsknechts') and vengeful gentry from the countryside, he began by condemning the city fathers for their inaction. Then he took the initiative. He gave Kett one last chance. On August 24, his herald approached Mousehold with an offer of pardon. According to a later chronicler, hostile to the rebels, at Kett's headquarters the herald denounced the rebels as "scumme of the people". He was confronted by "an ungracious boy, who pulling down his breeches, shewed his bare buttocks, and did a filthy act". One of the herald's party shot the cheeky lad dead; in the ensuing uproar any chance of peace disappeared. Now the final, tragic chapter in the tale began. The rebels withdrew from Norwich, using captured artillery to bombard the city from the heights. Warwick's professionals, who had initially been hampered in messy street fighting, went on the offensive. The decisive battle took place at a site identified as Dussindale. The exact spot is unclear, and is open to debate. It is unlikely the battlefield was at the modern estate near Thorpe St Andrew, now called Dussindale. Latest evidence points to an area around Silver Road and the Magdalen Gate, slightly downhill from the original rebel camp. Disciplined artillery, cavalry, gunners and pikemen shattered the rebels, who fought bravely for up to eight hours. Clearly this was no disorganised rabble, but an organised force. Nevertheless, up to 3,000 of them died. Kett fled, but was soon captured. Warwick showed no mercy. Many prisoners were hanged outright in the marketplace; Kett and his brother William were found guilty of high treason. Robert was hanged in chains from Norwich Castle on December 7, William from the tower of Wymondham Abbey. Warwick deposed Somerset, but he was later executed by Queen Mary. For over a century a service of thanks for Kett's defeat was held at St Peter Mancroft Church, Norwich. Kett's reputation was restored by 19th century radicals, while in the 20th century Labour-voting Norwich hailed him as a working class hero. He was an honourable man, but out of his depth. In trying to restore the balance within a divided society, he got more than he bargained for.

Burning of Francis Kett

In January 1589, a 42-year-old doctor and Cambridge University graduate followed in an unwanted family tradition. Dr Francis Kett met his maker in Norwich – at the site where his more famous uncle had perished.

Kett. . . that's a familiar name

As we saw in the previous chapter, uncles Robert and William Kett, of an old and prosperous Wymondham family, led a famous Norfolk rebellion back in 1549. Robert and William were executed, but their brother survived. Thomas Kett, born in about 1500, presumably took no part in the uprising. He and his wife Agnes had a young family to think of; son Francis was about two years old at the time.

A troublesome lot?

The Ketts had always been a respected, conservative family, and their involvement in rebellion was out of character. The harsh treatment dished out to rebels served its purpose as a deterrent. Norfolk never showed any kind of dissent afterwards, and all was quiet during the reign of Queen Elizabeth I, which began in 1558. Thomas Kett died five years before that, and his widow remarried Stephen Verdon. He helped finance young Francis Kett's education. In 1566, aged about 19, he entered Clare College, Cambridge, as a sizar – a student of limited means who paid lower fees than wealthier students. Four years later he emerged as a Bachelor of Arts. He must have been a keen student, as he stayed on a further three years to take his MA, became a fellow of the college and was at some point ordained – so he could, had he chosen, have taken up a career in the Church. The only mention of him during his college years was as a signatory on a letter thanking Elizabeth's chief minister, Lord Burghley, for help given to the college. Burghley was closely linked to Cambridge, it being his former university.

All very orthodox...

If Francis Kett's career had gone rather smoothly to date, in 1580 came the first sign that all was not well. Francis resigned his fellowship, and a year later became a doctor. In a time of turmoil many educated people were being influenced by new ideas in religion. And new ideas, in the time of the Tudors, could get you into serious trouble. Some have suggested Kett got involved with the poet (and possible spy) Christopher Marlowe, who held unorthodox ideas on most things. However, as their times at Cambridge barely overlapped, it seems unlikely. Kett published one work on theology. Entitled The Glorious and Beautiful Garland of Man's Glorification, it was orthodox in views and dedicated to Queen Elizabeth. Published in 1585, it ruffled few feathers. However, in 1588, the Bishop of Norwich, Edward Scrambler, dropped a bombshell. He accused Kett of heresy. In a document entitled Articles of Heretical Pravity, he accused Kett of Arianism and millenarianism. Being an Arian meant Kett denied the divinity of Jesus. The Christian Church had struggled with this contentious issue for centuries, ever since the time of Emperor Constantine in the fourth century AD. The orthodox opinion was that Jesus was divine. Other views were heretical, and dangerous. According to Bishop Scrambler, Kett believed Jesus "suffered only as Jesus already and shall suffer hereafter as Christ". Millenarian sects believed the end of the world was just around the corner, and that Jesus Christ was going to judge everyone on earth for their behaviour. They were very much on the far left of Puritan thought, and were a headache for the Church and secular authorities. A Norwich minister, William Burton, weighed in. He claimed Kett believed that "Christ is not God, but a good man as others be". Burton added: "Monstrous as he was in opinions, see how holy he would seem to be in his outward conversation. . . the sacred Bible almost never out of his hands, himself always in prayer, his tongue never ceased praises of God."

Benefit of the doubt, maybe?

Heretics and dissenters were giving the government all sorts of troubles. The Elizabethan regime was in a mood to crack down. While Catholics were already in their sights – particularly in the wake of the Spanish Armada which menaced England that summer – troublemakers from the Puritan side were also concerning them. In Norwich in the early 1580s, two radical clerics, Thomas Harrison and Robert Browne, had set up an independent church in Norwich, whose views were troubling the establishment. Burning heretics was nothing new in Norfolk. Early Protestant reformer Thomas Bilney, a university graduate and cleric like Kett, had been executed back in 1531 before the Reformation. He had been burnt at the traditional site, Lollards Pit, outside the city walls on what is now Riverside. During the reign of Queen Mary, Protestants had been persecuted. Conservative Bishop Hopton had nearly 50 people put to death, including Cecily Ormes, an artisan's wife from Norwich. The early years of Elizabeth's reign had seen a reduction in the number of executions, with the newly established Church of England trying to tread a middle course. But the times were changing. Religious positions on all sides were more extreme, ideas were hardening – and so were hearts. In 1583 two members of Browne's congregation were arrested for selling copies of his incendiary publications. They were hanged. In Kett's case Bishop Scrambler had seen and heard enough, and clearly regarded him as a threat. On October 7, 1588, he wrote to Burghley, urging him to execute Kett as a dangerous heretic. Sure enough, on January 14, 1589, he was burnt to death in the ditch at Norwich Castle.

Nasty business. . .
William Burton witnessed his death, and left a scarcely believable account of Kett's death. "When he went to the fire he was clothed in sackcloth, he went leaping and dancing. Being in the fire above 20 times together clapping his hands, he cried nothing but blessed be God, and so continued until the fire had consumed all his nether partes and until he was stifled with the smoke." Francis Kett, like many before and after him, paid a high price for his beliefs in a time when religion was all-important.

Educating Norfolk

"The Norfolk lads, I am sore afraid,
Have overmuch liberty".
With these words, Sir William Paston founded his grammar school at North Walsham.

What did the Norfolk lads think?

They were far too busy conjugating their verb tables to be able to give an opinion, but we were to hear plenty more from Sir William. His move to found a school in north-east Norfolk came during the golden years of the grammar schools' foundation. A tradition of education had existed among the clergy. Cathedral and monastery schools had taught young boys – and it was almost exclusively boys – since medieval times. At the Reformation most of these institutions bit the dust, and it seemed there would be a void. Quickly this vacuum was filled as grammar schools sprouted across the country, often on ground previously occupied by religious institutions. The reign of King Edward VI, whose Protestant government brought in much radical change, saw the first wave of grammar schools, and they continued into the reign of his sister Elizabeth and her Stuart successor, James I.

Who was Sir William Paston?

The Pastons had risen from humble origins in the late 14th century. From peasant origins they had risen to the ranks of the gentry. Generations of sons schooled in the law, allied to a steely determination within the family to hang on to, and expand, their lands saw the family prosper. They were important and influential in Norfolk. Sir William Paston was born into this family in 1528, and succeeded to much of the family estate following the death of his father and grandfather. A respected and generous man, he made weighty donations to his old university college – Caius and Gonville, Cambridge – as well as Norwich and Bath cathedrals, not forgetting

£10 a year given to the poor of Yarmouth and Caister. Knighted in 1578, he was a conscientious Justice of the Peace.

Why North Walsham?

Norwich and Aylsham already had grammar schools. North Walsham, the centre of the local wool trade, was close to the seat of the Pastons' wealth. It was logical, therefore, for this local magnate to endow a school in his own neighbourhood. There is a suggestion that there had been trouble in the area. Just half a century earlier some North Walsham men had joined Robert Kett's 1549 rebellion. And during the Peasants Revolt of 1381, a North Walsham man, Geoffrey Lister, had led his own uprising in Norfolk. Perhaps it was felt the area could do with some more peaceful influence. The town had suffered a major disaster in 1600. A terrible fire had destroyed much of its centre, burning down homes, stables, warehouses and malthouses. Many people were left homeless and ruined. The fire did leave plenty of empty land to build upon. Two years after the disaster, Sir William bought a plot and the school began to take shape. It probably consisted of a central room with a dwelling for the Master. Soon, amid ringing of bells, feasts, toasts and much fanfare, it opened.

Only for the rich, no doubt!

Education was provided free of charge by the philanthropic Sir William. Sons of the gentry sat down alongside farmers' and shopkeepers' children. In theory, the very poorest labourers' sons could have attended, but in practice they had to work from a very young age to help keep their families alive. It tended to be boys from the 'middling sort' who benefited from a grammar school education. Elsewhere in the country, a relatively well-off farmers' son like Oliver Cromwell at Huntingdon and an artisan's son, such as William Shakespeare at Stratford-upon-Avon, went to their local grammar schools. Similar lads attended Paston. They came from about the age of 10 and left at 14, though those destined for university might stay until 17. Many Norfolk youngsters went on to Caius and Gonville, the

'Norfolk' college at Cambridge. On October 1, 1606 the Paston School officially opened, and it is this date which is remembered as its birthday. It was designed for a maximum of 40 boys enrolled at any one time. Some, from the surrounding countryside, boarded in town. It was stipulated in Sir William's Founding Deed that pupils should be taught free of charge from the "hundreds of Erpingham, Tunstead, Happisburgh, East and West Flegg". Names of the earliest pupils have been recorded. They had surnames familiar in the area for generations; Robert Flight, Henry Scarburgh, Edmund Suffield and Andrew Doughtie to name a few.

What was taught?

As the name suggests, it was grammar and not much else. Latin grammar, to be precise. The school curriculum was nothing if not persistent. The lads who their elders felt had too much 'liberty' were drilled in Latin from 6am in the morning in summer (7am in winter) and went on until 5pm in the afternoon following a two-hour noon break. Discipline would have been pretty stringent in keeping with the views of the era, with beatings fairly common. As Sir William phrased it, in the school's Deed, the boys should also learn: "Good manners, learning and the true fear, service and worship of Almighty God, whereby they might become good and profitable members of the Church and Commonwealth." The school was to turn out good citizens as well as good scholars. There was time for "sport and recreation" in the school's adjoining playground.

Who did the teaching?

Michael Tilles was another Cambridge graduate, the grandson of the Vicar of Burgh. Although he had a clerical education he was not ordained. Aged 44 when the school opened, he had nine children of his own and had previously worked as a private tutor. Although Sir William's word was law – and he was to be the sole examiner of the boys' and the masters' work – Mr Tilles was an influential man. He was paid a salary of £20 a year. An Usher, paid £10 a year, was also appointed. Salaries were paid twice a year, and stayed the same until 1760, by which time the money was not quite so attractive. Sir William also appointed a paid lecturer to deliver a talk once a week, a post which remained intact until the late 1600s. The school took as its emblem a heraldic griffin above six fleurs de lys and the motto "*De mieux en mieux pour tout*" – From good to better everywhere.

A thriving institution?

Aided by the Paston family the school taught local boys for generations. The institution survived the death of its founder. Sir William himself died just four years after founding his school, and was buried in North Walsham. He had a magnificent alabaster and marble tomb made in the town church. His successors continued to patronise the school. The family continued to prosper despite backing the losing side in the English Civil War, joining the nobility as the Earls of Yarmouth, but their line died out in 1732. Mr Tilles remained Master until his death in 1625. Pupils included the likes of Horatio Nelson, who was taught there from 1768-71 before joining the Royal Navy aged just 12, and going on to a glorious career. During the 1980s the school merged with North Walsham High School for Girls to become a sixth form college. A further merger with City College Norwich took place late in 2017.

Both Sir William Paston and Michael Tilles were remembered in the school's song, an excerpt from which goes:
"Sir William Paston, he up and said
The Norfolk lads, I am sore afraid,
Have overmuch liberty
Come hither Rev Michael Tylles,
and into their heads we'll hammer
Godly learning to guide their wills
Arithmetic, writing and grammar."

The deserted village

An isolated remnant of a church tower in a field surrounded by sheep underneath a big Norfolk sky. What – and why?

A ghost town?

When Lord Justice Edward Coke bought the Norfolk village of Godwick in the late 16th century he built a barn and rebuilt the church tower in brick and flint. By that time Godwick no longer needed a church to minister to its flock, as the only flock in the village was just that. Sheep. They had replaced the people. But why? That remains something of a mystery. The peasants who once inhabited this piece of land a few miles south of Fakenham, and made a living of sorts, had no voice in their time. They have left little for us to remember them by now, save for the outlines of their humble homes – and a hint of just how tough their lives must have been.

How do we know the village was there?

Aerial pictures have shown up earthworks of a medieval village that existed, fluctuating in size and prosperity, for more than 500 years from Anglo-Saxon times. This and painstaking work by the Norfolk Archaeological Unit have helped historians build up a picture of a settlement mentioned in the 11th century Domesday Book. It had houses and gardens, along with a mill pond. The Church of All Saints, which is all that survives, would have been the focal point of a fairly elongated succession of cramped houses with small fields and strips of land. The self-sufficient peasant lived with his family and animals close at hand. Their houses were called 'tofts' or 'closes', and the boundaries can still be seen at Godwick, appearing as deep ditches. The windows were narrow and unglazed, little more than slits with wooden shutters. In their gardens they kept stock and grew vegetables. Beyond the village street they would have two or three strips they cultivated side by side with their neighbours, and from what they produced a proportion would go to the lord of the manor and the church in tithes. Other land was kept for hay meadow, plough land and woodland. The peasants ate unleavened bread, beans and hard cheese. Salted meat was a rare luxury. Clothes made of leather or wool would have to last a long time.

No wonder they cleared off! What was the land like for farming?
The village stands on a plateau of heavy, flat boulder clay soil. In heavy rainy conditions it gets quickly waterlogged, so a period of bad weather would mean deteriorating harvests. Marl pits, which still survive, were dug to improve soil conditions. By the mid-1300s a series of wet summers, the beginning of what has been termed a 'Mini Ice Age' in Europe, was reversing a period of growth. From the times of the Normans life had been relatively good, and marginal land had been brought under cultivation to feed a growing population. As life grew shorter and harsher, and many people died young from disease, the Black Death of the 1340s struck. It's believed between a third and a half of the British population died; we don't know exactly how many. The results were that many villages never recovered. Perhaps Godwick was hit by a combination of these factors. Then came the sheep. To rich landowners and merchants they were a source of wealth. To those on the bottom rung of society, a disaster. By the late Middle Ages it was more lucrative to farm sheep than have people working the land. Peasants made way for progress as a great deal of land in East Anglia was enclosed for sheep. By 1596, when it was recorded on an estate map, just three houses remained in Godwick and the church tower had collapsed.

Are deserted villages common?
It's estimated there are 200 such in Norfolk alone, though traces of most have been destroyed by ploughing. Godwick is a particularly good example because the land was never disturbed, except by the sheep. Examples near Fakenham include the evocatively named Pudding Norton and Little Bittering, mentioned in the Domesday Book

but gone by 1500. In Suffolk, West Stowe, near Bury St Edmunds, was an Anglo-Saxon settlement mysteriously abandoned. The East Yorkshire village of Wharram Percy, one of many deserted villages in that county, is today much studied by historians who lay the blame squarely on sheep farmers. Enclosure of common land for pasture was among the grievances that led to Robert Kett's 1549 uprising in Norfolk; like all such resistance, as we have seen, it was savagely crushed.

What about Edward Coke?

Judge Coke was a Norfolk man. Born at nearby Mileham, he made his name in the law courts of Elizabeth I. In 1580 he built a manor house at Godwick. It had a walled yard and entrance to the north and around the hall, a pattern of formal gardens and enclosures was laid out. It is believed the barn and church tower were incorporated into the landscape of his park; in effect they were ornaments in the landscape. The barn, now much altered with an elaborate facade, once reportedly had 200 men billeted during the reign of King Charles II, though what they were doing there seems a mystery. Coke's manor house lasted until demolition in 1962, and he was undoubtedly fond of it. During the 1620s he fell foul of James I, and was imprisoned in the Tower of London. He wrote praying he would be released to spend his last days at Godwick. As it was he was buried at neighbouring Tittleshall, with which Godwick was incorporated as a parish in the 19th century. The Coke family became agricultural pioneers and went on to inherit the title of Earls of Leicester, building the great hall at Holkham – as we will see later in this book.

What's at Godwick today?

Today the deserted village is part of a peaceful sheep farm. An agreement between English Heritage and the landowners means the public can visit Godwick between April and September, 9.30am until sunset. Information boards tell the tale; the rest is left to your imagination. The sheep seem unbothered by it all.

A troublesome priest

Who will rid me of this trouble-church Browne? (Queen Elizabeth I)

A maverick churchman with a powerful royal enemy. This sounds familiar.

Queen Elizabeth I's heartfelt plea echoed the words of her medieval ancestor Henry II. Unlike Thomas Beckett, Archbishop of Canterbury, Robert Browne was not destined to die a martyr's death. But it was no bed of roses for him. He spent much of his life in prison for his devotion to his faith (or trouble-making, depending on your point of view) and died in jail in his eighties. Some of his followers paid with their lives. Born into a wealthy family near Stamford, Lincolnshire, he founded an influential church at Norwich. It defied state authority, and helped inspire the Pilgrim Fathers in their move to America. His anti-establishment legacy may have spurred on his revolutionary American republican descendants a century and a half after his death.

How did he upset the queen?

Browne's upbringing was conventional enough. He was born at Tolethorpe Hall, Rutland, in about 1550, to a well-off and respected family related to their powerful neighbour Lord Burghley, Queen Elizabeth's chief minister. It was at university in the 1570s that he developed his radical ideas. Browne studied under the hardline Calvinist professor Thomas Cartwright at Corpus Christi college. This uncompromising puritan had great influence on Browne and his friend and fellow student, Robert Harrison, from Norwich. Both Browne and Harrison would soon be firebrand puritan preachers and teachers – and well on their way to clashing with the authorities. The queen and bishops were particularly sensitive to any criticism of the Church. Religious dissent threatened to boil over into civil war, as had been seen in France, so the authorities increasingly cracked down on it. Browne thought the Church of England established by Henry VIII in the 1530s was corrupt. Thus it needed 'purifying'. Thinking people should develop their own relationship with God, rather than rely on clergy to do the thinking for them, he wanted to see Church and State separated and bishops abolished. After teaching in Southwark, he took a curate's job at St Benet's Church, Cambridge. His views proved too strong for him to stay long, and he travelled to Norwich as Master of the Great Hospital. There he lodged with college friend Harrison. By now it was 1581 and Browne had already been jailed once. On this occasion it was for burning his licence to preach in Cambridge. Not for the first time it was his family connections with Burghley that got him released. In Norwich he and Harrison formed a church based on their own beliefs. This separatist body became known as 'congregationalist', and was to inspire others in the future. Many of the congregation were Dutch workers who had settled in the city to trade, usually in the textile business. Browne was busy publishing and preaching; once again he was arrested for unlicensed preaching at Bury St Edmunds, jailed and released.

Perhaps it was time to move on

In the early 1580s he and Harrison sailed to the Netherlands to join their former Cambridge mentor Cartwright and his congregation. The move went badly; each of these dominant personalities wanted to be top dog, and the three leading players soon quarrelled. Back in England Browne's writing, such as Treatise for Reformation, were declared heretical and banned on pain of death. John Copping and Elias Thacker, members of Browne's Norwich congregation, were arrested, tried and hanged for selling them in 1583. Browne, meanwhile, was on the move again. This time he went to Scotland. Surely this firmly Calvinist country would give him a welcome? Not quite. Soon, he was in trouble again. After being put under house arrest in Edinburgh, he traipsed across the land in an unsuccessful bid for converts. He became acquainted with some Scottish jails for his efforts. In all, this indefatigable character was imprisoned 32 times during his life. Exhausted and in ill health, he returned to his family in England.

They must have been delighted. . .

He was prosecuted for illegal publishing and preaching, then excommunicated. It may have been the shock of this and pressure brought to bear by his conventionally religious family, or perhaps his fragile health, that led him to abandon his radical beliefs. He recanted, promised to follow Church of England rules – and Burghley got him a job as a headmaster in Southwark. Later he took a church living as a vicar on Burghley's estate near Stamford. He lived there for the next 40 years, marrying twice, having nine children, and getting quite portly. After his second wife died and his children had all left home, he seems to have returned to his previous career. During the 1620s any puritans with separatist views were known as 'Brownists'; his reputation had spread. In 1633 he was summoned for non-payment of rates and reportedly struck the bailiff who delivered the summons. Jailed again, the 83-year-old was transported to Northampton jail on a cart with a feather bed on top. Like so many others, he died in prison of fever.

What was his legacy?

Like Robert Browne, the people who sailed from eastern England to America in 1620 aboard the Mayflower despaired of the Church of England. They set up congregationalist churches in America, and Browne is regarded as the 'father' of these Pilgrim Fathers. Among the early settlers were his Suffolk cousins. They dropped the 'e' from their surname once in the colonies, but did not drop their independent leanings. Solomon Brown, of Lexington, Massachusetts, is said to have fired the first shot that drew British blood in the 1775 skirmish there that sparked the American War of Independence. His first cousin, John Brown, was killed at Lexington. Solomon's brother, Captain Oliver Brown, led the pulling down of a large equestrian statue of George III the following year in New York. Separation of Church and State is enshrined in the US Constitution. These days Tolethorpe Hall is the scene of fresh dramas. It is the home of Stamford Shakespeare Company, whose excellent outdoor performances each summer draw thousands of visitors to the dogged old puritan's birthplace.

Kemp's Norwich dance

In 1600 actor and comedian Will Kemp danced from London to Norwich in nine days.

Why would he want to do that?

Today we would call it a publicity stunt. It would be covered on social media, probably accompanied by TV news crews. Will Kemp (or Kempe) was a contemporary and former colleague of William Shakespeare whose career was going through a bad patch. He later recorded his dancing odyssey in diary form, entitled "The Nine Days' Wonder" recounting his colourful and eventful journey. From that we have inherited the well-known phrase for a novelty which wears off quickly. Kemp was an accomplished comic actor, a celebrity in his time. The reign of Elizabeth I saw a flourishing of the creative arts, and there were a number of acting companies formed in these years. Born around 1550, he probably began his career as a member of the Earl of Leicester's company, but his name first appears after the death of Leicester in a list of players authorised by the privy council in 1593 to play near London. He is mentioned along with Shakespeare in relation to a company known as The Chamberlain's Men. In 1595 he appeared as joint payee, along with Shakespeare and actor-manager Richard Burbage, for plays enacted for the queen the previous Christmas. He may also have been a shareholder in the Globe Theatre. Kemp was a popular clown. Shakespeare, then in the early flowering of his creative genius, wrote such parts as the incompetent Constable Dogberry in Much Ado About Nothing and the quick-witted Touchstone in As You Like It specifically for Kemp. He may also have played Bottom in A Midsummer Night's Dream.

A slapstick artist?

He was described as "a shag-haired instrumentalist and dancer who could make a scurvy face and draw his mouth awry". His "mad jests and merry jigs" were ideal for comedy, but did not sit well with tragedy. Kemp felt there should always be a place for a comedy dog on wheels to provide much-needed laughs in a performance of Hamlet; Shakespeare disagreed. By 1599 his refusal to stick to the script led to a parting of the ways. They had "artistic differences".

Shakespeare sacked him?

That seems the likeliest explanation. But Kemp was a well-known figure, so his decision to take to the road – initially the result of a wager – in the spring of 1600 attracted a lot of attention. Kemp wrote up the story of his journey the following year – ostensibly to prove to his detractors that it was true. In his version, large crowds turned out to watch his progress for much of the 120 miles to Norfolk. With him came Tom Sly, his taborer (drummer), William Bree, his servant, and George Spratt, who acted as referee to confirm the journey was made. Although Kemp spent nine days dancing the journey actually took about four weeks, as he stopped off at inns and private houses along the way. He did not want for company. At Sudbury, for example, "there came a lusty tall fellow, a butcher by his profession, that would in a Morrice keepe mee company to Bury". Kemp was a morris dancer. This form of folk dancing goes back many centuries, and may have its origins in pagan agricultural ceremonies. It was certainly popular at the time, and would have been enacted at harvest time. Kemp's account relates the places at which he stopped. From Whitechapel, London, on day one he danced his way to Romford. After that his stop-offs included Chelmsford, Braintree, Sudbury, Bury St Edmunds, Thetford and Hingham before arriving at Norwich. At Bury he stayed for four days in an inn "by reason of the great snow that fell" before travelling over the heath to Thetford "dancing that tenne mile in three houres". It was not all easy going; the roads were pot-holed and Kemp suffered a sprained hip, but he was not about to give up.

What happened when he got to Norwich?

Kemp and his attendants reached the outskirts of the city on the

Wednesday of the fourth week. Being met by Roger Wiler, the mayor, he decided to spend the night outside the city gates at St Giles before a grand entrance could be arranged for the next day. Ever the showman, Kemp obliged with a fine performance. He eventually entered Norwich at Saint Stephens where, in his own words, there were "Wifflers (such officers as were appointed by the Mayor) to make me way through the throng of the people, which prest so mightily upon me". So great was the crush that when he tried to dance, he caught his toe in a girl's petticoat which fell off, to great amusement. After leaping over the churchyard wall at St John Maddermarket to avoid the crowds, Kemp was given the freedom of the city by the mayor and a grant of 40 shillings per year.

How did he follow that up?
Kemp later boasted that he had danced over the Alps. Although he was reported as performing on the Continent shortly after his Norwich feat there is no evidence of this. In 1602, a year before his death, he was a member of the Earl of Worcester's players, and stage manager Philip Henslowe's diary shows several payments made to him in that year. Sadly, his death went largely unrecorded, apart from a vague reference to the death of "Kemp, a man". It seems he had drifted into obscurity. Perhaps there was no longer a strong call for a talented comic with an amusing dog act?

Any critics?
Kemp complained of 'lyes' told about him by an "impudent generation of ballad makers and their coherents". Shakespeare's views on his erstwhile colleague are not recorded. A lifesize wooden sculpture of Kemp and his three attendants, commissioned by Norfolk Contemporary Art Society, is now in Chapelfield Gardens in Norwich. A wall plaque at the Maddermarket Theatre recalls his leaping feat. In modern culture, Kemp was portrayed in the 1990s cinema hit Shakespeare in Love, while Ben Elton's sitcom Upstart Crow featured Spencer Jones presenting him as a parody of avant garde comedians.

The Suffolk Leveller

"For really I think that the poorest he that is in England hath a life to live, as the greatest he... I think it is clear, that every man that is to live under a government ought first by his own consent to put himself under that government..."

With these words Colonel Thomas Rainsborough established his radical credentials. He acted as spokesman for thousands of people without an articulate voice of their own, particularly fellow soldiers from East Anglia alongside whom he had served. A distinguished English Civil War soldier and sailor, he had fought under Oliver Cromwell against King Charles I. He later became an MP, fighting a contentious election at King's Lynn in 1646. Before that Cromwell and Rainsborough had played a significant role in the Parliamentarian victory, but their ways would quickly diverge. When Rainsborough uttered his most famous words, he had just one year to live.

Who was Rainsborough?

Thomas Rainsborough has been seen by admirers as a courageous figure. He was certainly brave. Rainsborough (or Rainborowe) was the eldest son of the MP for Aldburgh, Suffolk, William Rainsborough. The family had strong links to the sea. William was a shipowner/master mariner as was his son. They were related to John Winthrop, the wealthy and influential Suffolk landowner who had founded the Massachusetts colony in 1630. Like Winthrop they were confirmed Puritans, and thus natural opponents of King Charles and his Archbishop of Canterbury, William Laud, throughout the 1630s. Thomas, born in about 1610 (the actual date is disputed) had spent time voyaging to New England, but on the outbreak of war in 1642 joined the Parliamentarian navy. As commander of the 34-gun frigate Swallow, he intercepted a Royalist vessel taking supplies to the king. He also played an active part in Parliament's defence of the vital port of Hull, leading a maritime raid by marines on the Royalist artillery which forced them to lift their siege. But there was more to Rainsborough than a naval commander. He transferred to the army of the Eastern Association, a move which led him directly into the orbit of Oliver Cromwell.

The Lord Protector. . .

Cromwell was just a cavalry commander at that stage, though the star of this Cambridgeshire landowner was rising. Rainsborough helped take Crowland Abbey from the Royalists in the spring of 1643, and also fought at the decisive battle at Naseby in 1645, he captured the important Royalist stronghold at Berkeley Castle and was present at a series of assaults on the king's fortresses. He was just the sort of "plain, russet-coated captain" that Cromwell liked. Oliver also liked Rainsborough's religion. Like Cromwell he was an 'Independent', one of the growing numbers of men in the Army and elsewhere who not only rejected the traditional Church, but also called for freedom of conscience. Which was not what everyone in Parliament was fighting for. When one of its leading commanders, the Earl of Manchester, declared: "If we beat the king 99 times he is still the king; if he beat us once we will be traitors and like to be hanged" he was expressing the conservative, limited war aims of many in Parliament who wanted to preserve the status quo. To Rainsborough and many of the New Model Army soldiers – men like Col John Okey, the dragoon commander of humble origins and Col Thomas Harrison, the son of a yeoman – this was not enough. As the war dragged on through the 1640s they and some of the troops under them became more radical.

A revolution?

The unofficial spokesman of the Army radicals – the Levellers as they became known – was John Lilburne. An astounding, fearless character, Lilburne left the Army and called for a whole new social order. Parliament should be dismissed, declared 'Free-born John', and re-elected every two years on a basis of almost universal (male) suffrage, the law courts should be abolished and re-formed. Rainsborough agreed. In 1647, with the king a prisoner and Lilburne imprisoned by Parliament in the Tower of London, Rainsborough was a frequent visitor. By now discontent within the Army was rife, and many were calling for action. The positions of each side were articulated at debates held that autumn. In the chancel of St Mary's Church, Putney, from October 28 to November 11, the Levellers had their say. One of their foremost spokesmen was Colonel Rainsborough, the highest ranking Leveller in the Army. Cromwell chaired the debate, and tried to follow a moderate course. But he was a man of property, and the Levellers' 'one man one vote' demands went too far. His point of view was put by his son-in-law, Henry Ireton, who argued with Rainsborough. It was at Putney that Rainsborough made the speech quoted on Page 118.

What happened next?

Rainsborough was now an MP. His first attempt at election to Parliament had ended in failure. At King's Lynn in January, 1646 he alleged malpractice by the mayor to defeat him and see a Royalist-inclined candidate, Edmund Hudson, elected. But, then, Lynn was always a Royalist town, and Rainsborough was an outsider. The following year he was more successful, elected MP for Droitwich, Warwickshire. He was thus in an ideal position of influence as battle lines were being drawn in Parliament, with the threat of mutiny in the Army. Rainsborough returned to the Navy, but at the outbreak of a second civil war his crews mutinied and he was put ashore. Reconciled to Cromwell, he rejoined the Army and helped take Colchester from its Royalist defenders. In October, 1648, he was sent to Doncaster to join the siege of Pontefract. Four Royalists, with a forged message from Cromwell, gained entry to his billet and tried to abduct him. It is believed they wanted to exchange him for a Royalist prisoner, Sir Marmaduke Langdale. Rainsborough resisted, and in a fight in the street was killed. His subseqent funeral in London turned into a mass demonstration by the Levellers. Some 3,000 mourners wore sea-green ribbons, adopted as the party's colours, in his memory.

England expects. . .

An English admiral from Norfolk fatally wounded in battle aboard HMS Victory. But this was not Admiral Lord Nelson in 1805; it was Sir Christopher Myngs 139 years earlier.

Another Norfolk hero?

Christopher Myngs' life story reads like an adventure book. Born in a Norfolk village in about 1625, he went to sea, reportedly as a cabin boy, became a buccaneer on the Spanish Main, was knighted for valour in battle – and died fighting for his country. Yet he was not entirely a dashing figure; more of an old sea dog, he had his critics, from Spain to Jamaica, and was more fondly remembered among pirates of the Caribbean than he was at court in London.

Humble origins?

Myngs was born near Blakeney sometime between 1620 and 1625 (the date is disputed) and it was Samuel Pepys who span the tale that the admiral began life at sea in a humble station. It's certain he was not born with a silver spoon in his mouth. By the time he commanded HMS Elizabeth in 1648, he was an experienced hand. In the first Anglo-Dutch War (1652-54) he was at the fore, capturing ships as prizes. In 1655 he was appointed captain of the Marston Moor. The crew was close to mutiny, but Myngs seems to have been a canny operator, and took control. He took the ship to the Caribbean, where he commanded the Royal Navy flotilla. Any mutinous thoughts his crew may have harboured soon disappeared as they reaped the rewards offered by prize money. England was at war with Spain, and the fleet took to commerce raiding. Myngs was particularly enthusiastic, getting a reputation for brutality. The Spanish claimed he was a pirate who sacked towns and massacred whole populations. Summoning privateers such as Henry Morgan – government-licensed 'legal' pirates – he raided Spanish colonies along the South American coast.

Hero – or villain?

Edward D'Oyley, governor of Jamaica, reckoned he was the latter. In 1660 he accused Myngs of corruption, and sent him under arrest back to London. The newly restored monarch, King Charles II, sent him back to Jamaica, with orders to carry on pillaging. This he did, seizing Santiago de Cuba with a privateer army 1,400 strong. Officially, the government in London deplored his excesses; unofficially, they sanctioned them. Wounded in battle, Myngs returned to England and was in an ideal position when a new Anglo-Dutch war broke out. On June 13, 1665, the two equally matched fleets clashed 40 miles off Lowestoft. A combined total of more than 200 ships and 43,000 men met in a hail of gunpowder and fire that would see up to 3,000 dead in a single day. It ended in a decisive English triumph, the fruits of which would be squandered amid political infighting.

Politics is a dirty game. . .

Cromwell's Commonwealth had bequeathed a powerful Navy. The king gave command to his brother, James, Duke of York. Prince Rupert of the Rhine, uncle of the king and formerly a dashing Civil War cavalry commander, led one squadron; Edward Montagu, a former Parliamentarian now reconciled to the monarchy and ennobled as Earl of Sandwich, commanded another. Sandwich, a Cambridgeshire landowner with an impressive estate at Hinchingbrooke, near Huntingdon, had given a vital job at the Navy's London headquarters to a hard-working young clerk. He was Samuel Pepys, whose diary is an invaluable guide to Restoration England. Pepys recorded his frustrations with the inefficiency and corruption which blighted the Navy. The Royalist commanders depended on the old 'tarpaulins' (tars), such as Myngs, who served directly under Rupert.

Time for action

The Dutch had a fleet of 103 ships, with 4,869 guns and 21,613 men; England had 109 vessels, 4,542 guns and 22,055 sailors. At first light the Dutch attacked, under their admiral, Jacob van Wassenaer Obdam. It was a confused melee; individual captains attacked independently. When it came to a fleet battle the English had the upper hand; their guns were heavier and more powerful than the Dutch. After several hours' sparring, the English flagship Royal Charles, with the Duke of York on board, duelled with Obdam's flagship, Eendracht. James narrowly avoided death when chain-shot decapitated some of his officers, then Eendracht exploded. Obdam and all but four of his crew were killed. The Dutch second-in-command, Kortenaer, had already been mortally wounded. The battle was now a series of close-quarter melees, causing horrific casualties on ships. The leaderless Dutch faltered and many captains fled. Edward Barlow, a young sailor under Rupert's command, described the Dutch, "seeing their Admiral lost, began to turn their arses and run". The English gave chase. And then stopped. Some said the Duke of York lost his nerve; others said his wife had told officers to keep her husband safe, and they gave the order to halt the pursuit. At all events, the English let their beaten rivals escape. Lowestoft was a great English victory. They sank 17 Dutch ships and killed up to 2,500 men with 2,000 prisoners; England lost just one ship, with 800 killed. "Great news, at last newly come," wrote Pepys in his diary. "We have totally routed the Dutch."

And Myngs?

Knighted for his heroism at Lowestoft, he and England looked set to reap the rewards of victory. But the Navy failed to blockade the Dutch in their ports, and they regrouped under new commanders. The following year Myngs took part in the massive North Sea battle known as The Four Day Fight. Aboard HMS Victory, he was wounded by a shot from a Dutch sniper in the rigging of an opposing ship. Although he survived long enough to be taken ashore, Myngs soon died. The war ended the following year with the Navy in disarray. A third war broke out in 1672. Another battle was fought off Southwold – a bloody draw in which Sandwich was killed. The Navy became more professional, evolving into the peerless force which eventually boasted the likes of Horatio Nelson, a sailor in the mould of Christopher Myngs.

The unlucky Cavalier

"I have been dealt an unlucky hand."

So wrote Sir Roger L'Estrange of his chequered life and career. He was a Royalist in the civil war, then a discredited and penniless exile, subsequently the government's chief censor and, finally, an embittered ageing Cavalier.

Chequered, indeed.

Roger was one of three sons of Sir Hamon L'Estrange, whose family had been important landowners at Hunstanton for several generations. Old Sir Hamon was an impressive figure, learned, courteous and widely respected. The family's misfortune was to live in interesting times. By 1643 war had been raging for over a year between King Charles I and Parliament. In Norfolk things appeared quiet. The Puritan party was strong in East Anglia, dominated by the likes of Oliver Cromwell and the Earl of Manchester and organised as the Eastern Association. Local Royalists were cowed and intimidated. Among their number were the L'Estranges. Not that they kept their feelings secret. They had faced financial penalties due to their "malignancy" and were in dispute with many neighbours. When, in August 1643, the Duke of Newcastle's Royalist army advanced west of the Wash in the direction of Norfolk, the Royalists rose up.

Led by L'Estrange?

The only member of the family with any military experience was Roger. Aged 27, hot-headed and impetuous, he had, like Oliver Cromwell, been educated at Sidney Sussex College, Cambridge. He had fought with the King's army during the disastrous "Bishops War" against the Scots in 1639, when an inexperienced and unpaid English army had been soundly beaten. Now he helped his father and brothers, Nicholas and Hamon, in seizing the port of King's Lynn. They hoped to hold it until relieved by the Marquis of Newcastle's forces. It was a well-organised coup. According to later Parliamentary reports, Sir Hamon had assembled 1,200 muskets, 500 barrels of powder and 40 cannon. But Cromwell, then a cavalry Colonel, anticipated the danger and reacted quickly. Seizing West Lynn across the river, he set up batteries to begin bombarding the Royalist positions. By the time the Earl of Manchester took over the siege and the Parliamentary navy blockaded the port, there was no sign of Newcastle's relieving force. By mid-September the besiegers prepared to storm the town. But Manchester saved further bloodshed by offering to release the garrison unharmed if they surrendered. The month-long siege came to an end.

But not the bitterness
Before long the family's local enemies were persecuting them for wrongs done during the siege, leading to financial ruin. Roger was far from beaten though. Joining the king in Oxford, he persuaded him that Norfolk was full of Royalists just waiting to rise again. Charles gave him a commission. The following year he was back in west Norfolk, trying to seize Lynn once more. Soon he in peril. Roger contacted a sea captain called Leaman who he thought reliable, but was betrayed. Arrested, he found himself accused of spying. During the civil war there was a fine line between espionage and military activity, and L'Estrange appeared to have crossed it. The civil war was becoming particuarly bitter by late 1644, when L'Estrange was tried at the Guildhall, London. Condemned as "a Spy and treacherous conspirator, in endeavouring to betray the Town and Garrison of Lynn", he was sentenced to die. But for once he was fortunate. Appeals for his life to the civilised and humane Earl of Essex fell on sympathetic ears, and he was instead imprisoned at Newgate. There he stayed for three years. Roger still had plenty of fight left in him, despite the surrender and imprisonment of King Charles. In 1648 L'Estrange was released (or escaped, by his own account) and was in Kent when a second civil war broke out. Caught up in the fighting – by some accounts he actually instigated a premature local rising – it ended badly when the army

crushed it. Within weeks he was a fugitive in exile, denounced by friend and foe alike for his ill-judged actions. His reputation was harmed by this and his later clash with Edward Hyde, Earl of Clarendon, the young King Charles II's chief adviser and spokesman for the Royalist cause. Roger lingered in the Netherlands, living on dreams and promises for five years, returning to England in 1653 shortly before his father's death. His father, "overpowered by the times" had retired to Hunstanton after the siege of Lynn to live quietly.

Surely Roger did well after the Restoration of Charles II?
Not half as well as he would have liked. He became a self-appointed spokesman for old Cavaliers who wanted full compensation for their sufferings during the war and under the Commonwealth. But Charles II and Clarendon pursued a more moderate course, trying to reunite the country and avoid another war. Royalist veterans like L'Estrange were not satisfied; hard to blame them after all they had been through supporting the cause. He was a ready convert to the Tory party that emerged to support the future James II during the Popish Plot of the 1670s, and became well known for denouncing the opposition Whigs in a series of polemical pamphlets. Diarist Samuel Pepys called him "a man of fine conversation. . . most courtly and full of compliments". Roger thrived under James II, becoming Surveyor and Licenser of the Press as well as MP for Winchester. The wheel turned again in 1688 when William of Orange replaced James in the Glorious Revolution. Roger lost his offices, and retired to Norfolk in straitened circumstances.

Any time for a private life?
He married late, aged 60, to the much younger Anne Doleman, from a Whig family. Perhaps inevitably it did not work well, though the couple had two children. His daughter broke his heart by converting to Catholicism; Roger remained an Anglican until his death, aged 88, in 1704. He had indeed been dealt an "unlucky hand" – though he had not always played his cards well.

The

Georgians

King's Lynn Customs House, with the great 18th century explorer George Vancouver's statue in the foreground. Customs and excise officers tried to keep smugglers in check during the 1700s.

An explorer and his cat

In the Lincolnshire village of Donington stands a statue. It depicts a man in naval uniform, complete with telescope. At his feet plays a cat. Matthew Flinders remains more famous on the other side of the world than he is in his homeland. As does his cat.

Any connection to Flinders Park tennis venue in Melbourne, Australia?
The same connection to the Flinders River and Flinders mountain range Down Under. Matthew Flinders was an explorer, born on the edge of the Lincolnshire fens but near enough to the coast for the sea to beckon him. His navigational skills, courage and sheer endurance made him the ideal man to name a whole continent. At a time when Britain produced superb sailors, Flinders gained himself a posthumous reputation to rival

Explorer Matthew Flinders

that of the likes of his near contemporary James Cook. His name seems better known today in Australia, where it has assumed near mythical proportions. At sites such as Hervey Bay, Queensland, and Western Point, Victoria, there are many Antipodean coastal lookouts named after Matthew Flinders.

What was his background?
Flinders was born at Donington in 1774. The son and grandson of doctors, he was not marked out for a career at sea. But reading Daniel Defoe's Robinson Crusoe as boys, he and his brother Samuel were hooked. For contemporary heroes they needed look no further than Cook, whose voyages of the 1770s were inspirational. Against the initial wishes of his father, who wanted him to follow in his footsteps,

Matthew sought advice from his uncle John, who was in the Royal Navy. Aged 15, he joined HMS Alert as a lieutenant's servant. Later he sailed with one Captain William Bligh. Bligh became notorious due to the Mutiny on the Bounty, but Flinders got on with him better than Fletcher Christian, who led the infamous uprising against his captain in 1789. Sailing aboard HMS Providence, Flinders, by now a midshipman, and Bligh reached Tahiti on a voyage intended to take breadfruit as a crop to the West Indies. This time there was no mutiny; Bligh, who knew a thing or two about navigation at sea, recognised he had a first class young explorer aboard. Flinders' career blossomed.

Navigation was all very well, but weren't we at war with the French?
War was to have a huge impact on Flinders' life and career. In 1794 he fought as a midshipman aboard HMS Bellerophon as the Royal Navy crushed its French counterpart at the battle known as the Glorious First of June, off Ushant, near the French coast. But he was to have no Nelsonian career as a fighting sailor; within two years he returned to the part of the world that had captured his youthful imagination. He sailed with Australia's governor John Hunter to the penal colony at Port Jackson in New South Wales. The mysterious continent – barely known and still unnamed by Europeans – was a blank canvas as far as mapmaking went. Flinders set about filling in the blanks. Along with his friend, ship's surgeon and fellow Lincolnshire man George Bass, he started recording the coastline in intricate detail. In a series of intrepid voyages the two adventurers made charts for the area around what is now Sydney. They sailed in a tiny open boat called Tom Thumb, then proved that Van Diemen's Land (now Tasmania) was an island, by sailing around it. This knowledge greatly helped navigators by saving them from having to go all the way around Tasmania. The passage between Australia and Tasmania is today named Bass Strait.

Adventurous, certainly, but dangerous work
On one occasion the two explorers encountered bemused Aborigines. To defuse a tricky situation Flinders produced some scissors and began

cutting their hair to amuse them. Later, while Flinders returned to England, Bass sailed into the Pacific bound for South America – never to be seen again. Despite much speculation, his fate remains unknown. Back home, Flinders married vicar's daughter Ann Chappell in 1801. His long suffering father was once again taken by surprise, writing in his diary: "Matthew came home suddenly and unexpectedly, with a wife, a Miss Chappell. I had no notice of intention, I am seldom consulted by my young folk, except on the need for raising money for them." Matthew was soon keen to finish the job he had begun Down Under. This time he approached one of the greatest scientists of the day. Sir Joseph Banks, another Lincolnshire resident, had sailed with Cook years before, and used his influence to help Flinders take command of HMS Investigator. His greatest voyage was about to begin. Refused permission to take his new wife along, he left her behind, and reached the south-west coast of Australia in December, 1801. Flinders wanted to produce comprehensive maps of the whole coastline of Australia. With him went brother Samuel as navigator, botanist Robert Brown, illustrator Ferdinand Bauer along with an astronomer, landscape artist and miner. But a French expedition was already there. Captain Nicolas Baudin had been sent by Napoleon to steal a march on the British. Inevitably the rival explorers met up in southern Australian waters. The two captains shared a personal and professional mutual respect, and even shared information. A short-lived truce had been declared between Britain and France, which helped matters. After parting company with Baudin, the Investigator became the first ship to circumnavigate Australia.

Job done. What could possibly go wrong?

Plenty. Leaving the damaged Investigator at Sydney, Flinders was first shipwrecked on the Great Barrier Reef, having to sail back in an open boat, then tried to hurry back to England by sailing in a tiny schooner. It was a fateful decision. Forced to seek help in French-held Mauritius in the Indian Ocean (where his friendly rival Baudin had recently died) Flinders was arrested as a spy. As war broke out yet again in Europe, he was held by the French for more than six years. By the time he was released his health was broken. He had just four years to live. At least he was reunited with Ann, and the couple had a daughter. In the time remaining to him Flinders wrote his Voyage to Terra Australis, and was the first to suggest the name Australia. He died the same day his book was published in 1814, and a few years later the name was formally adopted. As a new nation grew Down Under in the next century, so did his reputation there. More Australian places bear the name 'Flinders' than any other.

What about the cat in the statue?

Trim the cat was born at sea in 1799, and named after a character in the book Tristram Shandy. As a kitten he fell overboard, but swam back to the ship, then scaled a rope to get back aboard. Impressed by his determination, Flinders and his crew adopted this lucky black feline with white paws and chest. The captain described him as "one of the finest animals I ever saw". Trim sailed around Australia with Flinders on his epic voyage, and survived the Great Barrier Reef shipwreck. Later he shared the captain's Mauritius imprisonment, but poor Trim disappeared there – believed eaten by person or persons unknown.

Anything else?

Flinders' daughter Anne married and had a son. Sir William Flinders Petrie was a renowned archaeologist and Egyptologist. Saint Mary's Church in Donington has a display dedicated to Flinders, including a stained glass window and a first edition of his book. His brother Samuel is buried in the graveyard there. In January 2019, an archaeological dig near Euston Station, London, opened a new chapter in the story. In preparation for the new HS2 rail line, graves were exhumed in St James's Garden. Among the remains of thousands of people buried there, a lead plate placed on top of a coffin identified it as that of Captain Matthew Flinders. Appropriately, there is another statue of him at Euston Station. At time of writing, his remains were due to be interred at a fresh location.

'Turnip' Townshend

The man who introduced turnips to Britain?

Not quite. Revisionist historians have been chipping away at 'Turnip' Townshend's reputation as one of the founders of the 18th century Agricultural Revolution. Perhaps in the past there has been an over-concentration on the influence of individuals, but there is no denying this Norfolk man's place in the story of agricultural reform. He helped increase productivity and popularise the 'four-field' rotation system. Yet Charles Second Viscount Townshend would probably be amazed to be remembered as an agricultural pioneer; the nickname 'Turnip' was originally applied ironically to a man who had held high office before his top-level political career was ended by a family row.

Whig or Tory?

The Townshends were 'natural' Tories. Descended from a long-established county family who had risen along with the Pastons under the Tudors, their family seat was at Raynham in west Norfolk. Charles's father had supported Charles II, and such fervent Royalists were usually Tories. Thus it was that when Charles, educated at Eton and Cambridge, entered Parliament in 1701 it was as a Tory. Perhaps repelled by the extremism of the party under Queen Anne (they swayed towards belief in the divine right of kings and suppression of religious dissent), he switched to the more liberal Whigs. After a period in charge of the Yeomen of the Guard his first big break was as joint peace negotiator with the Duke of Marlborough. Britain had been at war with France since 1702. Marlborough's string of continental victories at such places at Blenheim and Ramillies had brought glory, but war weariness set in after more than a decade of conflict. Most people were keen for peace. A period on the continent put Townshend in the perfect position to launch a political career. The Hanoverian Elector George was about to inherit the British throne from the childless Anne via his Stuart grandmother. King George I spoke no

English and knew little about the country he was about to rule. Townshend and the Whigs offered him a warm welcome, plus political stability. On his arrival in England in 1714 George appointed Townshend Secretary of State for the Southern Department – in effect in charge of foreign affairs. Townshend was able to name his Chancellor of the Exchequer; his brother-in-law, Robert Walpole.

The future prime minister?

Just another Norfolk squire at the time. The two families were prominent in county politics, and it was only natural that Townshend should marry Walpole's sister Dorothy in 1713, following the death of first wife Elizabeth. This East Anglian 'mafia' was now taking over the government of the country. The two men had a lot in common, bluff, hearty squires fond of country pursuits and their food and drink. Townshend's critics dismissed him as "coarse, rustic, and seemingly brutal". These were not his opponents, the Tories, but his fellow Whigs. Politics was a rough business; a successful practitioner kept his friends close, and his enemies closer. The wily Earl of Sunderland had wormed his way into King George's confidence, and succeeded in getting Townshend and Walpole sacked in 1716. Townshend was offered the poisoned chalice of the Lord Lieutenancy of Ireland. Eventually he accepted – as long as he did not have to set foot in that country! Unsurprisingly, he was soon dismissed. The wheel quickly turned; within three years the ministry of Sunderland and Earl Stanhope was rocked by the South Sea Bubble financial scandal, for which they were blamed. The way was clear for the Norfolk duo to save the day. Walpole took over the financial reigns at the Treasury, and Townshend returned as Foreign Secretary.

A happy partnership?

Walpole liked to say that, as long as the 'old firm' of Walpole and Townshend were in charge, all would be well. The two thrived; peace abroad and prosperity at home were their watchwords. They easily survived the death of the king in 1727 and continued in power under his successor, George II. The Treaty of Seville in 1729 guaranteed peace between Britain, France and Spain. But there were jealousies between the two, as in so many political partnerships. When Dorothy died in 1726 much of the glue that had bound them together was loosened. A minor issue caused a breach; when Walpole refused to appoint Townshend's friend Lord Chesterfield to office they quarrelled; only the intervention of friends stopped them coming to blows. In 1730 Townshend resigned to spend more time on his country estate.

And discovered turnips!
They had already been imported to Britain as cattle fodder since the 1670s. Townshend divided his fields into four different types of produce with wheat in the first field, clover (or ryegrass) in the second, oats or barley in the third and, in the fourth, turnips or swedes. The turnips were used as fodder to feed livestock in winter. Clover and ryegrass were grazed by livestock. He grew more crops and got a better yield from the land. If a crop was not rotated, then the nutrient level in the field – and thus yield – would go down. In this way, the land could be "rested", and also improved by growing other crops. Clover and turnips grown in a field after wheat, barley or oats, replaced nutrients into the soil. None of the fields had to be taken out of use while they recovered. Townshend was not the first to use this system, but he did make it popular. More crops grown meant more people could be fed; thus the population grew. The nickname 'Turnip' probably came about due to sarcastic urbanites like the poet Alexander Pope, who mocked him as being obsessed with turnips.

I'm sure turnips are very interesting. Anything else?
Townshend died of apoplexy in 1738. In an age in which politicians were notoriously corrupt he made little money, and left his 12 children ill provided for. His wife Dorothy is said to be the 'Brown Lady' – the ghost who haunts Raynham Hall. His grandson, 'Champagne Charlie' Townshend, had a disastrous political career in the 1760s, helping to spark the American War of Independence with unwise tax policies.

The 'in' place to be

Kingdom, the TV series starring Stephen Fry as a solicitor, put Swaffham firmly on the tourist trail. But this attractive Norfolk town has a long way to go before it matches its 18th century appeal, when life centred on its large market place.

A popular spot?

Today's market place looks much as it did during the 18th and 19th centuries. Apart from the heavy traffic that afflicts the town centre, the likes of Admiral Lord Horatio Nelson, Methodist founders John and Charles Wesley and Robert Walpole's sporting grandson would probably feel quite at home. They were just a few of the gentry and leaders of local society who enlivened Swaffham's social life during the 'season'. For a while this spa town with a reputation for healthy living became the 'in' place for Norfolk's upper crust to see and be seen. This is reflected in the distinctive Georgian architecture still visible.

A town with a long history?

Founded by Anglo-Saxons, by the time the Domesday Book was compiled in 1086 Swaffham had a population of fewer than a hundred. A settlement stone to the north of the market place, on Lynn Road, is said to have been put there by fifth century pagan settlers. Swaffham's position at a crossroads on the routes through Norfolk east-west to Yarmouth and north-south to London brought it to prominence. The large triangular area in the centre of town lent itself perfectly to fairs and markets. Henry II granted two charters to the town in the 12th century while following the granting of a third charter in 1215, the town was allowed to hold a market and three fairs per year there. The fairs were held on May 12, July 21 and November 3, when sheep, cattle and other livestock were brought to be traded. As late as the early 20th century schoolchildren got a half-day holiday on these fair dates. Swaffham's golden age came during the Georgian period of the 18th century. Many of the outstanding buildings around the market place date from this time. The Assembly Rooms were built in 1775, and became popular locations for balls and other social events. Nelson, on his rare home visits from duties at sea, attended. His wife Fanny lived in the town while her husband was at sea, and it is believed she lodged at elegant Montpelier House, in modern Station Street. Another Assembly Rooms regular was Lady Caroline Townshend, a society beauty and trend-setter from the renowned Norfolk family. They were not alone. Many influential Norfolk families took houses in the spa town at certain times of the year. A very significant figure in Swaffham's history was the third Earl Orford. George Walpole was the grandson of Robert, Britain's first Prime Minister, whose family seat was at Houghton Hall. Orford was a profligate rake, but also a well-liked county figure as he preferred living in Norfolk to going down to London. His passion was sport. He had long enjoyed the town's racecourse, and it was in the Greyhound Inn, close to the Assembly Rooms, that he and his friends created the town's Greyhound Coursing Club.

A real sporting gent. . .

Orford was also responsible for the town's iconic market – or butter – cross. A cross had stood on the site from at least the 16th century, marking a place where people would gather for trade. In 1783 Orford paid for the distinctive modern structure. It is an elegant domed building supported by eight Doric columns. In keeping with the Georgian passion for subjects based on classical ancient civilisations, it was topped off by a figure of the Roman goddess Ceres. She was the goddess of fertility and agriculture, and from her name is derived our word 'cereal'. Appropriate in an area which relies heavily on the production of cereal crops. Originally a butter market was held there (hence the name) which continued until the mid-19th century.

Anyone else of interest?

It wasn't just aristocrats and gentry who patronised the town. Dotted around the market place are references to an important figure in the 18th century Evangelical movement. John Wesley, founder of the Methodist Church, preached at Westgate House from an upstairs window when the congregation from the chapel became too large and spilled outside. The house was owned by a Methodist family, the Goodricks. On the other side of the market place stands the site of the town's former grammar school. Nicholas Hamond, described on a plaque outside the house as lord of the manor, was the founding father, leaving £1,000 for the school's creation. Now relocated, the school is known as the Nicholas Hamond Academy. Following a destructive fire in 1775 a number of properties had to be rebuilt. The town hall, now a museum, was among those. Today the museum has exhibits depicting the social history of Swaffham and surrounding villages, as well as a display devoted to Howard Carter. Born in Swaffham, he was the Egyptologist who discovered Tutankhamun's tomb.

How long did the good times last?

Swaffham was still thriving in the 1840s. In William White's 1845 History, Gazetteer and Directory, it was described as "one of the handsomest and busiest market towns in the country, and the principal place for election of knights of the shire". Later in the century the town went into decline. Life had never been easy for the poor agricultural workers who made up most of the population, and a depression in farming hit hard. Emigration and a drift to towns in search of work saw the population drop from 3,858 in 1851 to 2,600 in 1931. The town has recovered since, and new uses have been found for many buildings. The Assembly Rooms, used by American GIs as a canteen during the Second World War and later for meals by Hamond's schoolchildren, has been restored to its former glory as part of the Iceni Partnership Regeneration Project, complete with glittering chandeliers and oil paintings. It is used for conferences and exhibitions. The town's Victorian Corn Exchange, where corn was sold on market days and local farmers would congregate to do business and socialise, has been converted to modern use.

A palace fit for a duke

"When I am in the tennis court of my palace in Norwich," said the Duke of Norfolk, "I think myself as great as the king".

Some palace – some duke!

Thomas Howard, third Duke of Norfolk, was quite a character. The king's Earl Marshall, commander of his army, leader of the conservative faction at court and uncle of Anne Boleyn, he was a powerful figure at the court of King Henry VIII. Members of a Norfolk family who had come to local prominence in the 1400s, the Howards spent much of the 16th century coveting power at Westminster. But they never forgot their East Anglian roots, being major landowners and powerbrokers in Norfolk and Suffolk. Such local magnates needed a suitably grand headquarters in England's second city. Norwich. Where else? In 1540 the duke set up his town house in what was to become Duke Street. There's no sign of a Tudor palace there now. We'll never really know just how grand the palace was – it was largely demolished 300 years ago. Recently though, excavations have given us more clues to the scope of the palace.

A home fit for a duke . . .

The palace on the banks of the Wensum wasn't the first grand city house the family built. Mount Surrey was constructed near former monastic land at the top of St Leonards Hill to the east of the river. The Earl of Surrey, the duke's brilliant poet son, started building it in 1544 in the Italianate style then becoming popular. Surrey also put up a house closer to the centre of Norwich; called Surrey Court, it was in what is now Surrey Street. All was going smoothly for the talented 30-year-old Howard heir, but it rapidly went horribly wrong. Paranoid and ageing Henry VIII had him executed on what looked like a trumped-up charge of treason in 1547; two years later Robert Kett's rebels sacked Mount Surrey, of which not a stone remains. His father, that great survivor of Tudor politics, sold Surrey Court – today the Norwich Union (Aviva) building is on the site. It was left to Surrey's son, who became the fourth duke following the death of his grandfather, to lavish money on the Norwich palace. It too was built in Italianate style in the form of a quadrangle with a court in the centre and an entrance in the middle of the south side. Sports fans would have no cause for complaint – the palace housed a bowling alley and covered tennis court. The north and south ranges were three storeys high, the other two boasted four. Before long the palace was the largest private house in the city. Not everyone was impressed. Thomas Baskerville said it was "seated in a dunghole place" surrounded by tradesmen's and cloth dyers' houses on the other side of the river.

Just no pleasing some people!
In 1671 the palace entertained its most distinguished visitor. King Charles II, restored to the throne a decade earlier, came to Norfolk to reward the loyal and build bridges with former enemies. Apart from knighting the distinguished Norwich antiquarian author and doctor Thomas Browne, whose statue stands today on Hay Hill, he also stayed at Blickling Hall with former Parliamentarian Baronet Hobart, and at the palace with leading Royalist, Lord Henry Howard. His elder brother, the duke, was insane and lived abroad. The Howard family had only recently been restored to the title, having forfeited it on the execution of the fourth duke for treason a century earlier under Elizabeth. For too long they had been under a cloud because of their adherence to Catholicism in Protestant England, and the visit of a hopefully more tolerant monarch was a coup. Charles stayed at the palace along with the usual extended – and expensive – entourage that monarchs brought with them. The queen alone brought 55 people, and many had to be housed in the tennis court.

Grand palace, visiting royalty. . . how did it all go wrong?
The glory days of 1671 were a distant memory 40 years later. In 1710, amid fears of Catholic Jacobite mobs rioting in the city, the mayor of

---

Norwich, Thomas Havers, refused the duke permission to hold a processional entry. He feared pro-Catholic unrest in a city where feisty apprentices were prone to the odd riot or two. The duke was outraged. Almost at once he severed links with Norwich, and ordered the demolition of the palace. The site went into a long decline. He let one wing to the city to use as a workhouse, where conditions left much to be desired. In the later 18th century and first half of the 19th, unemployment in Norwich was rising. Numbers fluctuated, but as many as 1,200 people out of a population of about 30,000 might be in the workhouse at peak times. Overcrowding became scandalous. More than one inmate committed suicide. Visiting journalist James Neild wrote in 1805: "In the first room I visited there were 42 beds, ten of them cribs for single people, and the others had two in each, there being 74 persons in this room". Although the Poor Law guardians rebutted these charges, which were published in the Gentlemen's Magazine, charges like this helped bring about gradual change. The building was falling apart; in 1739 three children died when a wall in the palace yard fell on them. Its days were numbered.

And today?

In modern times the site has been used as an electricity works, a brewery and a multi-storey car park (rebuilt a few years ago), and now luxury apartments are being built there in a part of the city where rebuilding seems to be reaching new proportions. A Catholic chapel survived until the 1960s as a billiard room before making way for the car park. Some years ago archaeological excavations were undertaken before housing went up. They uncovered six-foot deep foundations, part of a flint wall, along with evidence of earlier industrial activity at the site. It appears there was a 13th/14th century cloth-dyeing business, and 12th century quarry before the palace was built. What more surprises will the Duke's Palace reveal? Hopefully, these finds will enable archaeologists to give us a fuller story.

■ The title of Duke of Norfolk remains in the Fitzalan-Howard family.

A walk on the wild side

In 1751 a wanderer arrived in Norwich. Unable to speak, he was initially treated with suspicion. It was just one episode in the strange – and rather poignant – tale of Peter the Wild Boy.

Something of a mis-spent youth?

Found in the wild, and believed to have been reared by animals, Peter's true identity remained a mystery for his whole life. He went from a minor celebrity at the court of a king to a neglected figure who died in obscurity. But his tale caught the imagination, along with other stories of 'feral' children. They both repelled and fascinated the civilised world. You only have to look at stories such as Rudyard Kipling's Jungle Book, featuring Mowgli, the boy brought up by wolves, or Edgar Rice Burroughs' Tarzan, Lord of the Apes, or even go back into ancient history to the legendary foundation of Rome by Romulus and Remus – said to have been suckled by a wolf – to recognise the lasting appeal of these legends. Peter was the real thing. A boy brought up in the wild by animals. Or was he?

Where did he come from?

In 1725 hunters in the German forest of Hertswald, near Hameln, discovered a strange boy. Naked, walking on all fours, he was wary of people. This "brownish, black-haired creature" would run away and climb up trees to escape when approached. Aged about 12 years old, he could not speak – or at least form coherent human words. Soon he came to the attention of Duke George of Hanover. He also happened to be George I, king of Great Britain since 1714, but at this time at his court in Herrenhausen. Peter, as the wild boy was dubbed, was treated as an honoured guest. Dressed in fine clothes, he got to sit down with the king. Unsurprisingly, his table manners left much to be desired. Peter refused to eat bread, instead gorging himself on vegetables, fruit and barely cooked meat; he particularly enjoyed asparagus. He declined to use cutlery, eating out of his hands noisily. In fact, like an animal. The king and his court decided he had never been among people before, and he was ordered to be taken away and educated.

Never to be seen again?

To their credit the royal court continued to treat Peter humanely. Caroline, Princess of Wales, took a shine to him. She persuaded her usually grumpy father-in-law to take him back with them to England. There his celebrity grew. Although he insisted on sleeping on the floor, Peter was given a tailor-made suit of red and green. London society was soon agog with his antics. "There is scarcely talk of anything else," wrote the author Jonathan Swift. Philosophers and anthropologists were fascinated by Peter. In this new Age of Reason, as the early 18th century was known, there was much argument about the 'noble savage' being somehow better and intrinsically more natural than civilised humanity. They watched his progress with interest, expecting great things of him as his education advanced. The king chose one of the best tutors he could find to civilise the wild boy. Dr John Arbuthnot (1667-1735) was a leading Scottish physician, mathematician and scientist. Both were given rooms at Kensington Palace, and lessons began in language and manners. "Dr Arbuthnot showed care, skill and tenderness," but Peter made poor progress. He could do little better than manage words of one syllable, though he did learn manners such as how to bow and kiss fingers. The call of the wild was still strong; he had a "natural tendency to get away if not held by his coat". Peter's fifteen minutes of fame were soon up. Society gossips quickly found new diversions and the philosophers were as disappointed in him as were his teachers. Within three years Dr Arbuthnot declared he could do no more.

Back to the forest?

Peter was sent to live on a farm near Northchurch, Hertfordshire. Granted a decent pension of £35 a year by the Crown, he was certainly not abandoned, but was largely forgotten. The tendency he had shown earlier to wander off became more pronounced as he got older. He would walk for miles. But Georgian England held greater dangers than the German forests. In 1745, during the Jacobite Rebellion, as Bonnie Prince Charlie's army marched as far south as Derby before retreating, Peter was arrested as a suspected Highland rebel, and lucky not to be shot. Six years later came his celebrated long walk to Norwich. There, his inability to speak other than a garbled form of the words 'King George' got him arrested as either a vagrant or, worse, a foreign spy. With Britain frequently at war with either France or Spain, it was a dangerous accusation. He was locked up in the Bridewell prison for a while until a representative of the king heard of his troubles and came to release him. After that he was fitted with a collar introducing him as "Peter, the Wild Man of Hanover. Whoever will bring him to Mr Fenn of Berkhamsted shall be paid for their trouble." Peter lived on until a respectable old age, finally dying in 1785. We can only hope he found some kind of happiness in a world he surely could not understand.

So, who was he really?

Peter has continued to fascinate and mystify. The early ideals of him being a 'noble savage' with innate wisdom and leadership qualities, such as the mythical Tarzan or Kipling's Mowgli, have been tarnished by suggestions he was in fact mentally retarded, abandoned by his exasperated parents into the wild. His inability to grasp the concept of speech is held to signify that he had the mind of a toddler. Or could it be that he had missed out on the vital early socialisation when, as very young children, we learn speech and other characteristics from parents? Nobody can say for sure. In Norwich, The Wild Man public house in Bedford Street, just around the corner from the Bridewell – itself now a museum of social life – is named after its briefly famous visitor. Peter and his tutor Dr Arbuthnot are immortalised in a series of pictures of real life people painted on the grand staircase at Kensington Palace by the artist William Kent in 1726. Perhaps his life, and his fleeting fame, tell us a lot about the fickle nature of celebrity – something we hear a lot about in the modern world.

Smugglers' yarns

Five and twenty ponies, Trotting through the dark –
Brandy for the Parson, 'Baccy for the Clerk,
Laces for a lady; letters for a spy
And watch the wall, my darling, while the Gentlemen go by.

Rudyard Kipling's verse reflects the romance, mythology and danger of smuggling. But it was a business – and a brutal one at that.

Spirits, tobacco and tea. . .

Ever since King Edward I introduced Customs duties in England in 1275, people have been trying to get around them and provide products that are heavily taxed to customers at a fraction of the cost. In the Middle Ages it was wool and hides that were smuggled; by the 1700s it was spirits, tobacco, tea and silk. Although we think of Cornwall as the hotbed of smuggling East Anglia's long coastline, with its inlets and quiet beaches, were fertile ground. The waterways of the Broads proved an ideal inland distribution network, with wherrymen happy to add a little contraband to their cargo. By land, ancient footpaths such as the Peddars Way were used, and the curious deterred by dissemination of legends about the likes of Black Shuck haunting the route. The area around Massingham became known as The Smugglers' Way. In the 18th century a war went on between the authorities and the smugglers. Many people sided with the criminals.

Perhaps they were just scared!

The smugglers were often armed and ruthless. In the long-running battle with the Revenue men of the Customs and Excise, it was often the smugglers who came out on top. The heyday of the smuggler was the 1700s. In 1688, the government extended Customs duties to a number of products that had previously been lightly taxed or not at all.

What had been a haphazard way of collecting duties now became formalised, but without effective policing the law was frequently flouted. To ordinary people these taxes were unfair and exorbitant. Those 'gentlemen' who broke the law and engaged in what became known as 'free trade' became, to some, heroes, or at least acceptable. On the government side, ports such as King's Lynn and Great Yarmouth were bastions. At Yarmouth the Revenue's fleet tried to detect, catch and prosecute smugglers. At Old Hunstanton there is a memorial to two men. William Webb, a trooper of the 15th Dragoons, was shot by smugglers on September 26, 1784, while Revenue officer William Green "in the faithful discharge of his duty was inhumanely murdered by a gang of smugglers". Two of the gang were captured, but two Lynn juries acquitted them of the crime. King's Lynn's Custom House was the centre for the Revenue men where, in theory, all duties were paid. A staff of officers, from a Controller, the top official, to landing, coast and tide 'waiters', checked shipping. They were on the front line. Records tell of some 250 officers "beaten, wounded and abused" between 1723 and 1736. In 1718, for example, Revenue men fought a pitched battle at a house in Lynn where smugglers had hidden contraband brandy. The Revenue men had their successes. In December, 1801 two Excise men and a detachment of Dragoons fought smugglers at Horsford; one soldier was shot, while two smugglers were killed and several wounded. Then in 1832 Brancaster officers seized 5,565lbs of tobacco and 650 gallons of brandy and gin from a large tugboat.

Who were the smugglers?

Many places have smuggling legends. John Dunn, the Stiffkey smuggler, once landed on Wells beach with his gang while a horse race was going on there. The smugglers outnumbered the Revenue men, who called upon a militia officer who was taking part in the race, Major Charles Loftus, to help. The major led a charge against the smugglers, but they escaped. In January, 1743, a naval scrap took place off Mundesley between a Revenue smack and a smuggling vessel. With nine guns to the Revenue's three, the smugglers outgunned their pursuers – and had time to taunt them as they sailed off. The area between Weybourne and Sheringham was good for smuggling, as it afforded good landing spots, while Happisburgh manor house was said to be a smuggling headquarters. Gangs hunkered down at places like Sea Palling and Blakeney. One of the most dramatic battles was between the Revenue cutter Ranger and a well-armed smuggling vessel. The chase began at Robin Hood Bay, Yorkshire, and ended off the coast at Yarmouth. After an exchange of gunfire the smugglers abandoned ship, leaving a large cargo of contraband gin, tobacco, tea and silk. Two smugglers and three government men died, with seven wounded. Despite a reward of £500 offered, the surviving smugglers were never caught. Richard Wiseman, of The Three Pigs, Edgefield, provided an alibi in 1807 and was acquitted, while Cawston smuggler Jeremiah Abel was found guilty. Significantly, these cases were heard at the Old Bailey, which implies a local jury would not convict. Many winked at the trade. Weston Longville vicar James Woodforde was as respectable an establishment figure as you could hope for. Yet, his diary records casually that: "Andrews the smuggler brought me this night a bag of Hyson tea. . . he frightened us a little by whistling under the parlour window just as we were going to bed". The parson also bought "Moonshine" gin and brandy from the local blacksmith, John Buck. In 1792 Buck was 'informed' upon and found with contraband – but got off with a small fine. Although penalties for smuggling were harsh, they were not always enforced.

This couldn't go on

Following the end of the Napoleonic Wars in 1815 a period of peace meant less had to be spent on the military, so the government cut taxes. The philosophy of free trade was in the ascendancy, so customs duties were gradually cut. Law enforcement became more organised, with the introduction of the police force in the 1830s. Today, smuggling continues in such fields as drugs and people trafficking, though shorn of its glamour and most public support.

The landscape genius

Humphry Repton was the man who invented the art of landscape gardening

Hang on, wasn't that Capability Brown?

Repton would have been the first to acknowledge the huge debt he owed to his hero, the legendary Lancelot 'Capability' Brown, who was about 30 years his senior. Born at Bury St Edmunds in 1752, Repton was marked out from youth as a businessman but instead pursued a career in botany. From the late 1780s onwards he treated gardening as an art form and made a business out of it.

In the 18th century it was a rich man's game

It's true that most of Repton's clients were wealthy – as had been Brown's – but he helped publicise the benefits of a beautiful garden for lots of more humble folk. Humphry Repton's career was one of contrasts, from Norwich textile merchant to a leading politician's election manager, playwright to professional gardener, he turned his fertile mind to many pursuits. His father John, a prosperous excise collector, moved with his wife Martha and three children to Norfolk from Bury St Edmunds when Humphry was 10. After the boy had spent a spell at Norwich Grammar School Repton senior decided his son's career was to be in exporting goods to Holland, then a vital part of the Norwich economy as ships could navigate all the way up the Yare and Wensum into the heart of the city. To that end 12-year-old Humphry was sent off to study in Holland and learn Dutch. The chances are that is where his interest in gardens may have been sparked, for the Dutch were great horticulturalists. "A Dutch merchant's accounts and his garden were kept with the same degree of accuracy," he later said. Returning to England four years later Humphry was set up in trade by his generous father. Things did not go that well, what with ships being lost at sea, and the death of both parents proved the last straw. Humphry moved with his new wife Mary to live in the country. At Sustead near Aylsham he took up the study of botany and entymology along with his Norwich friend James Edward Smith, later to make his name as first president of the botanical Linnaean Society. With time for reading and writing he published a History and Antiquity of the County of Norfolk (1781) and lived the life of a country squire. He made friends with his landlord William Windham, of nearby Felbrigg Hall, and became his election manager. A close ally of Prime Minister William Pitt the Younger, Windham was posted to Dublin as Lord Lieutenant of Ireland. Repton, with a growing family, was in need of money so went with him as confidential secretary – his business manager in other words. As it happened it was a short-lived appointment as Windham quickly resigned his post, but Repton stayed long enough to make some useful contacts. When he returned to England he moved to Essex and began his landscape gardening career in 1788. After writing to a number of the influential people he met in Ireland, Repton offered his services as an 'improver of landscape' on their English estates. Soon he was in work, his first job being for silk merchant and Norwich mayor Jeremiah Ives at Catton Park, then just outside Norwich. With his enthusiasm, business sense and wide learning Repton made a science of gardening. He is credited with inventing the term 'landscape gardening'.

Did he do the digging himself?

More of an ideas man really, rather than a 'hands on' digger. For each of his works Repton drew up a 'red book', volumes created for each client, with finely drawn before-and-after maps, mathematically correct illustrations, watercolours, and ideas for changes to the gardens. These volumes were then bound in red leather and presented to the client. He charged five guineas a day plus expenses, with a fifty per cent discount for Norfolk customers. From the 1780s until his death in 1818 Repton was a leading figure in creating fashionable gardens. Although he undertook fewer large-scale developments than Brown he had more than 400 smaller projects. Among his credits are Sheringham Park and

Woburn, one of the great English parks. He also drew up red books for features at Felbrigg Hall and Holkham in Norfolk. Woburn and Welbeck are probably his greatest works. The landscape was his canvas, requiring "the united powers of the landscape painter and the practical gardener", he said. Repton introduced gravel walks and brought back separate flower gardens. He also replaced classical ornaments with romantic structures like grottoes and fake ruins. Aristocrats liked to guide their visitors around their estates, constantly surprising them with the variety around them. Repton, like Brown, liked using the natural beauty around him and disapproved of trying to recreate Italian scenes then in vogue. He was in many ways a conservative.

What did he do at Sheringham?

Repton drew up a red book for new owner Abbot Urcher: "I hope I may be allowed to indulge my favourite propensity for humanising as well as animating beautiful scenery". By now working with his son he designed the house and the park, contrasting garden and park with wild landscape. The house is sheltered and the park looks out to sea. Sadly, Abbot Urcher never lived to see the finished project; he died tragically young. His successors created the brilliant rhododendron and azalea gardens which enchant modern day visitors to this National Trust property. It links to the Norfolk coast path to make a memorable day out.

Any critics?

Gardening was now a competitive market, and Repton drew fire from more radical designers. He never quite made it into the same league as Capability Brown by becoming George III's 'Gardener Royal'. Nor did the Prince of Wales accept his architectural proposals for building Brighton Pavilion. He did get a mention from Jane Austen in Mansfield Park (1814), in which Mr Rushworth's ancient estate is being 'modernised'. A coach accident in 1811 left him with spinal injuries which consigned him to a wheelchair, and curtailed his life and career.

The boy prodigy

He was the child genius from a humble background who went on to shine as a Cambridge don – and have a literary law named after him. Richard Porson was born on Christmas Day, 1759, in the village of East Ruston, near North Walsham – but his academic fame was to spread far and wide.

Nature or nurture?

Huggin Porson was the parish clerk of East Ruston, his wife Ann Palmer a shoemaker's daughter from nearby Bacton. Porson senior was a worstead weaver who succeeded his father as parish clerk, while his wife learnt to read and write while in service in the house of a gentleman. As parents they were ahead of their time in their love of learning. Together they produced highly intelligent children – boys and girls – though Richard proved the most talented. In an age when few people from poor backgrounds managed to thrive in the rarified world of English academia, he proved an exception. At their cottage home, the children had few advantages. Their parents could not afford many books, except for some works on mathematics, and the Bible, of course. But their father drilled them on classes after school, so they had plenty of support at home.

Plenty of support at school?

The Porson children were remarkable. At their village school in Bacton, John Woodrow was the first to spot their phenomenal memories. At a time when there was no compulsory education, the sons of the rich had private tutors, better-off lads went to grammar school, while boys from modest backgrounds got basic education at village schools. Girls, if they got any learning at all, received it in the home. For the most part it was classics – Latin and Greek – and mathematics on the menu. Fortunately for Richard Porson, he excelled in both. At his second school in Happisburgh, on the Norfolk coast, schoolmaster Mr Summers declared the three brothers were the brightest boys he had taught in 50 years. His sister Elizabeth also displayed academic talent, but never got much chance to use it. Finding Richard could work out cubic roots in his head, Mr Summers said he was "shrewd, sensible and intelligent". Bacton vicar Thomas Hewitt was his next patron. He educated the 11-year-old Porson at the vicarage along with his own sons for the next two years. To his earlier promise was added meticulous copying and skill in calligraphy. Norfolk could not hold the boy wonder. At the age of 14 he arrived at Eton.

Onwards and upwards?

Not quite. Porson went backward at Eton. Awkward mannered among the upper class boys he now mixed with, his natural abilities were allied to what seemed like laziness, which dogged him for the rest of his life. No-one doubted Porson's talents; he could show off his incredible memory from a young age, amazing all by being able to identify individual pages of voluminous Greek texts just by being told the quotation. Whatever his shortcomings at Eton, an academic career at Cambridge beckoned, and he entered Trinity College in 1778. There he specialised in Greek and literary criticism for over a decade. He was a renowned master of translation, with an international reputation. A witty, sociable man in company, he won friends and admirers. The convention was that scholars were ordained in the Church of England, but Porson shunned the established Church. His unconventional religious views got him into trouble; after one of his publications made fun of Christianity, a Mrs Turner of Norwich cut down a £30 legacy she had promised him. Porson had to earn a living, and a lay fellowship would have provided the means. He believed he had been promised this, but the master of Trinity gave it to his nephew instead.

A touch of nepotism perhaps?

No matter how brilliant you are, you need to have the right connections to get on. This incident seemed to sour Porson's view of

Cambridge. Although he was appointed professor of Greek there, he was not called upon to lecture or teach, and gravitated to London. There he struck up a friendship with newspaper editor James Perry of the Morning Chronicle. He married Perry's sister, Mary. The marriage may have turned out to have been a happy one, but Mary died within a year of the wedding. Porson reverted to his bachelor ways. From an early age he had a reputation as a heavy drinker. Even the notorious Lord Byron mentioned his "bestial intoxication" at Cambridge – which is setting the bar pretty high! Modern biographers believe this aspect may have been overplayed. That said, in an age in which alcohol consumption was heavy, a reputation like that had to be worked at. Porson could be forgiven for having a chip on his shoulder. He struggled financially; at one point his London friends raised £100 for his support, which he accepted only on condition he receive the interest in his lifetime and the rest be returned to the donors at his death. An appointment as librarian of the London Institution in 1806, at a £200 per year salary, also helped.

What about this literary law?

It may sound arcane to us now, but Porson's Greek scholarship was important. At a time when no man could be regarded as educated unless he read the classics, Porson's insightful work on writers such as Aeschylus, Euripides and Homer was influential. His 'law', concerning iambic trimeters – a device used in Greek tragedy and comedy – may only be relevant to pure classicists today, but it influenced many poets and writers who followed. Porson is remembered today with a Porson Prize for the best translation into classical Greek verse, awarded at Cambridge since 1817. Had he lived longer his already prodigious output would have increased. But in September, 1808, Porson had a fit while walking near the Strand. Unable to communicate, he was taken to a nearby workhouse. His friends, reading a newspaper report of a man found with scraps of Greek and algebra in his pockets, found him there. He died on September 25, aged 47 – his last words, appropriately enough, in fluent Greek.

An independent woman

Harriet Martineau was a woman ahead of her time. A fearless journalist and campaigner, she pioneered the cause of women's rights to lead an independent life – and was not afraid to make enemies.

As in Martineau Lane, Norwich, site of Norfolk County Council?
That's named after her brother, James, of whom later. Harriet was a Victorian rarity; a woman with an independent career. Like Florence Nightingale and George Eliot, she escaped the confines of a middle class upbringing to carve out fame in her own right as a campaigning journalist and writer on the issues of her day. Her influence spread from Britain to the United States. Harriet Martineau was born in 1802, sixth of eight children of a wealthy cloth importer of Huguenot (French Protestant) origins, Thomas Martineau, and his wife Elizabeth. The family were Unitarians, dissenters from the Church of England, but that was no impediment to their social standing. They were part of the elite of a city that was still significant nationally, though in economic decline due to war and competition from manufacturers in the north of England. Martineau had a difficult childhood, later describing it as a "burdensome experience". Prone to illness from infancy, she was deaf by 15, and was to suffer poor health all her life. Like many people so afflicted it made her more determined to be independent.

Not easy for a 19th century woman
Although her parents gave their daughters a progressive education at home, it was the boys who were earmarked for university and career. Harriet's destiny was to be marriage. Reluctantly, she became engaged to John Worthington. Despite writing anonymous articles for the Unitarian Monthly Repository, her future seemed mapped out. But in her twenties, Martineau's life turned upside down. First her father, then her elder brother, and then her fiancé died. The family fell on hard

times. While her sisters became governesses, Harriet's deafness made this impossible. Relishing the opportunity to make her name, she resolved to make a living from writing – and succeeded. Romantic novels of the Jane Austen type were not for this serious-minded character. Following a number of religiously inspired works, she published Illustrations on Political Economy (1832). It was a series of essays on politics and social reform, showing the influence of liberal thinkers like John Stuart Mill, and it established her reputation. At the time it sold more copies than Charles Dickens managed. The principles of political economy sought to encourage people to better their lot by self-help and education. Harriet was to write more than 1,500 columns as well as longer works and two novels. In 1832 she moved to London to further her career. Two years later she wrote supporting the Whig government's controversial Poor Law, and the implementation of workhouses for the poor. She took a liberal stand on issues from the repeal of the Corn Laws to the Crimean War. The income derived from writing gave her the independence to spend two years in the USA.

The land of the free?

Most commentators praised America's democracy, but Martineau was more critical. She backed the cause of the Abolitionists who wanted to abolish slavery in the USA, by then outlawed throughout the British Empire. It was not a universally popular stance to take in 1830s America, but Martineau was courageous enough to stand up for what she believed. Her second novel, The Hour and the Man, was about Toussaint L'Ouverture, the black slave who led an anti-colonialist revolt in Haiti during the Napoleonic Wars. She also criticised the USA's treatment of women, declaring in her Society in America that they were treated like "slaves". She argued for an improvement in women's education so that "marriage need not be their only object in life". Following the death of her fiancé, Harriet Martineau never married. She valued her independence, which in the Victorian age women often lost after marriage as their property was legally their husband's to control. In fact, she avoided close relationships for the rest of her life. "The older I have grown, the more serious and irredeemable have seemed the evils and disadvantages of married life," she later wrote. Her self-made wealth enabled her to build her own house in the Lake District at Ambleside in the 1840s. She was to spend much of her later life there. This followed several years' ill health when she was a virtual invalid, eventually cured by hypnosis. All this time she continued to publish on a variety of topical issues, although she was often housebound. Martineau was brought up in a religious family, worshipping at the Octagon Chapel in Norwich. Her younger brother James, to whom she was very close as a child, became a well-known cleric and philosopher. So it was a shock to all when, in 1851, Harriet renounced Christianity. It brought her some unpopularity, and led to a rift with her family, including James. In a deeply religious age that was to be rocked in 1859 by the publication of Charles Darwin's Origin of Species, such an announcement caused great offence. Her literary and political friends, such as William Lloyd Garrison, leader of the American Abolitionists, supported her though. She joined the staff of the London Daily News as a leader writer, enabling her to campaign for women's rights.

An early suffragette?
In 1866 she joined pioneering doctor Elizabeth Garrett Anderson campaigning for women to get the vote. She also attacked the Contagious Diseases Acts. This legislation was introduced to prevent venereal disease in the armed forces and enabled police in garrison towns and ports to arrest women they thought were prostitutes. Martineau was outraged as the acts applied only to women, and her opposition helped inspire Josephine Butler to head a campaign which led to the repeal of the acts in 1886. Martineau moved among the intellectual elite, such figures as Dickens, Thomas Carlyle and William Wordsworth – but in later life she suffered heart problems. Doctors gave her just a few years to live and she settled in her Lake District home, accompanied by two of her nieces. She died of bronchitis in 1876, aged 74. Today she is regarded as one of the first sociologists.

The 19th century

The Holkham Monument recalls the influential life of Coke of Norfolk, who died in 1842, and was given a grand send-off.

The Norwich School

In 1803 a group of artists met in a small room in Norwich. It was the start of a tradition that would last three generations and leave a lasting legacy.

Who were they?

The founding fathers were John Crome and Robert Ladbroke. They had met as teenage apprentices in Norwich. By 1803 both were in their thirties and established artists, though Crome was the more successful of the two. When they announced the establishment of a 'society' of artists they had a ready-made group of young followers ready to heed the call. By doing so they broke with a tradition in English art that drew talented hopefuls away from their roots to London. Norwich became the only regional school of painting ever formed in England. The country's second city, as it was at that time, had a strong cultural identity going back to the medieval period, when craftsmen created religious works. By the later 18th century it was home to philosophers, writers, musicians, scientists – plus art lovers and connoisseurs with the influence and wealth to encourage local talent. Such a man was Dr Edward Rigby. This art-loving philosopher in the 1780s employed a boy named John Crome to run errands. Seeing the lad had artistic talent he encouraged him and became a life-long patron. Rigby later introduced him to influential, art-loving Norfolk families such as the Norwich Gurneys, founders of Barclays Bank, as well as that of Great Yarmouth banker Dawson Turner. Crome later taught the children of both families, and even travelled overseas with them. As an apprentice his great friend was Robert Ladbroke, also a talented artist. The two young men rented a garret studio and encouraged one another's work. They later married two sisters, Phoebe and Mary Berney. It was logical that they should collaborate in 1803, when the first meeting of the Norwich Society of Artists was held at Little Cockey Lane, close to Castle Meadow.

Who else?

They were joined by a number of talented artists, some of whom were their pupils, including Robert Dixon, Charles Hodgson, James Stark, George Vincent and John Thirtle. The initial aims of the society were "for the purpose of an Enquiry into the Rise, Progress and present state of Painting, Architecture and Sculpture with a view to point out the Best Method of Study to Attain the Greater Perfection in these Arts". The president was elected by three quarters of members present, he appointed a vice-president and secretary, while new members also faced an election. The society met fortnightly. Two years later an exhibition was held in the city, when 18 professional and amateur artists showed off more than 200 works. It was such a success that it became an annual event, attended by Norwich's elite, until 1833.

Not everyone joined

Many artists showed their work, but never joined the society, which had 79 members at its peak. One big name missing in 1803 was that of John Sell Cotman. Cotman, regarded as an artist on a par with Crome, was trying his luck in London at the time. On his return to his native Norwich in 1807, he was invited to exhibit with the society. A few years later he became vice-president, and then president in 1811. Cotman produced what art historian Laurence Binyon, writing in the 1930s, hailed as "the most perfect examples of pure watercolour ever made in Europe", but he soon became frustrated in his native county. His avant garde style jarred with some contemporaries and he found it hard to sell his paintings, having to rely on teaching to make a living. In January, 1807, he advertised that he had taken a house in St Andrew's, giving lessons at £2 2s quarterly, and four private lessons at £1 1s. This was not a school in any formal sense, and had room for a number of different styles. Binyon characterised the Norwich artists as lacking any uniting theory, but there was a "deep unconscious bond between them, so that many a painting, though we may be at a loss to attribute it to a particular artist, is unmistakably recognised to belong to the Norwich school". Although the best known works, such as Crome and

Cotman's riverside, coastal and Broads scenes, feature Norfolk, the Norwich men also depicted scenes from elsewhere in Britain and scenes from abroad. The Norwich School specialised in landscape, which was popular at the time. Art historians at the Norfolk Museums and Archaeology service say the significance of the Norwich painters is in their realism based upon direct observation, and liken their work to that of the dominant figures in English art of the time, JMW Turner and John Constable. Constable was as inspired by the landscape of his native Stour Valley as were the Norwich artists by their own Norfolk homeland. Their work is contrasted to the perceived 'prettinesss' of Suffolk's Thomas Gainsborough and the 'classical' landscape inherited from the continental painters Claude and Poussin.

Any artistic differences?
In 1816 Crome and Ladbroke fell out. No-one is quite sure what prompted it; maybe a spat over amateur and professional membership, perhaps it was over money, it might have been that Ladbroke was jealous of his old mate Crome, who overshadowed him. Ladbroke broke away, joined by some other artists, and formed a rival grouping. The split lasted until 1821 when the two were reconciled on Crome's deathbed. By that time many of the artists had drifted back together, and many exhibited with both groups. A new generation thrived. Norwich art was a real family affair; Crome's son John Berney Crome (known as 'Young Crome' to differentiate him from his father, 'Old Crome') Stark's son Arthur, Ladbroke's son John Berney Ladbroke, and David Hodgson, son of Charles, were prominent. Joseph Stannard, born in 1797, was never a society member but his riverside and coast paintings were acclaimed. A third generation, including Stannard's son Alfred, and daughters Emily and granddaughter Eloise, who produced still life works, continued the proud tradition until the 1880s. Later Norfolk artists, including Alfred Munnings and Edward Seago, were influenced into the 20th century by Crome, Cotman and their followers. You can see many of the Norwich School of Artists' works on show at the city's Castle Museum and Art Gallery.

A day at the races

In June, 1841, a Dereham horserace winner celebrated in style. Not only did he win a large trophy, it was filled with eight pints of champagne. And subsequently refilled, and drained. Welcome to the convivial world of equine sport in 19th century East Anglia.

The sport of kings?

Kings, commoners and all sorts of people in between loved the sport in this era. Horseracing of any kind is an ancient pastime, and most likely predates the world's oldest civilisations. In England adoration of all things equine was particularly strong among the upper classes, who used horses both for war and recreation. It was the Stuart kings – James I, Charles I and in particular that Merry Monarch Charles II – who fostered horseracing. Newmarket in Suffolk was his turf of first resort. In 1675 it is said he actually rode a winner in a competitive race. You did not have to go as far as Newmarket though to watch, take part in or bet on the races. They could be virtually in your back yard, on the beach or on public roads.

A popular pastime?

The first recorded horse race at Great Yarmouth was in 1715, but there is little doubt these events began well before that. It was in this year that a group of innkeepers petitioned the town's Corporation for use of land at South Denes. The horses had to compete with other activities, such as donkey races and chasing a pig with a soaped tail. This latter event has, sadly, declined in popularity. Not so horseracing. At much the same time a course was established at Nacton Heath, near Ipswich, and flourished for nearly 200 years. By the early 19th century horseracing's appeal had spread to all classes, though it was the landed gentry who funded it and enjoyed the vibrant social life that went along with it. In September, 1811, for example, up to 20,000 people watched the annual September races at Great Yarmouth. "Most of the county families were present at the assembly," recorded the Norfolk Annals, an invaluable source of information. Even greater crowds assembled on Mousehold Heath, Norwich. In 1838 up to 30,000 fans flocked to the heath to watch the 'Coronation Races', so called to celebrate the crowning of Queen Victoria that summer. Like many of the meetings, these events could last two to four days, with a number of different races on the card. You didn't need to have a specialised racecourse prepared. In July, 1833, a flat race on the sands at Holkham was witnessed by some 10,000 spectators. When the tide began to come in, they adjourned to the hospitality tents, returning to the races when the tide turned. At Wells-next-the-Sea "an immense concourse of spectators" saw beach racing in July, 1818. Other races were held at places such as Blickling Park, Tivetshall, Swaffham, Mattishall, Cromer, Litcham, Downham Market and Thetford. Some owners made a name for themselves. In August, 1809, a purse donated by local citizens at Mattishall was won by a horse named Lord Paget, owned by a Mr Carter, "a well-known leader of sport in the district". John Harvey, Mayor of Norwich, was the man credited with promoting the sport in Norwich, though gypsies camping on Mousehold had been racing horses there for some time. Other horse lovers joined in. Cavalry regiments garrisoned at Britannia Barracks were, unsurprisingly, to the fore. In May, 1848, the 16th Lancers held their races at the Heart's Ease Inn, Plumstead, then part of the heath. Today the area is part of the Norwich ring road, another kind of race track. The following year, the troopers held their event at Stanninghall, near Spixworth. A Captain Lawrenson, of the 17th Lancers, was a winner at the North Walsham steeplechases in 1837.

Any champagne moments?

The sporting fraternity partied hard. In June, 1841, the ringing of church bells set off the sport at East Dereham's common. The cup was won by Mr Colman's Day Star. The trophy "weighed 41oz and contained eight pints of Howard's sparkling champagne, which the fortunate winner twice filled, and the company partook of it with true

English feeling". When Hector Munro's horse won a steeplechase from Fritton Church to Gorleston Church, he and his cronies caroused together at the Bear Inn. "The company were much gratified with an excellent local and appropriate song, the production of Mr Burton, of the Norwich Theatre Royal, and repeated by that gentleman in the course of the evening with increased effect." We can imagine. Race meetings were a chance for the county set to get together, dress up and enjoy themselves. In October, 1804, Lady Caroline Harbord held a ball and supper at Blickling to accompany the races there, attended by more than 100 guests from the Aylsham area. "A select party of 68 ladies and gentlemen" dined together at the Crown during the Swaffham Races of June, 1809, while 200 people danced the night away at the town's Assembly Rooms. At Cromer a new subscription room for dances debuted at the summer race meeting of August, 1814, attended by "many distinguished visitors", while East Dereham's 1824 event drew people of "beauty and fashion".

A leap of faith. . .
Originating in Ireland, where they know a bit about horses, steeplechases were originally defined by reference to church steeples, horses jumping countryside fences and ditches on the way. When, in 1832, Mr Charles Ellis, of Shelfanger Hall, saw his "celebrated little grey horse" beat a "grey mare of hunting celebrity", belonging to Mr Williams, of Diss, the race was between Gissing and Thurlton churches. Other steeplechase venues included Fakenham, Eccles, North Walsham and Barnham Broom. These courses tended to be over two to five miles. Rather longer were the trotting endurance matches. These were often held on turnpike roads. In 1833 trotters raced between Yarmouth bridge, Beccles and Halesworth, a distance of 25 miles. In 1810 John Chamberlain, of Magdalene, near King's Lynn, raced his horse Shales against Driver, owned by Reuben West, of Gaywood. With stakes at £200, they started from the South Gates, Lynn, and trotted to the nine-milestone on the Swaffham road and back. Shales completed 17 miles in an hour, and was the winner.

Any nasty shocks?

Surprisingly perhaps for the times, there was growing public disapproval of harm done to racehorses. In 1813 two animals were raced from Fakenham to Norwich and back again twice, a distance of 100 miles. One exhausted horse died, while the other was "much injured", leading the Norfolk Annals to complain of this cruelty. Similarly, 20 years later, Mr Gepps, of White Lion Inn, Beccles, for a wager of £200 drove his bay pony 100 miles in 12 hours from Harleston to Newmarket and back. "The wantonness of the act is much to be regretted," wrote the Annals. Interesting to note that the RSPCA was founded in 1824, getting royal patronage 13 years later. Passions could run high. In 1840 Norwich Mercury newspaper reporter Mr R N Bacon wrote that a rider "had too much nog in his head" when a horse named Newman Nogs fell at Long Stratton steeplechases and was destroyed. The jockey, William Bunting, took offence at this, and threatened to horsewhip the reporter at his office, while his employer, Captain Ives, "rode backwards and forwards in front of the office". A Norwich magistrate later bound Bunting over to keep the peace.

Was anyone having a flutter?

Oh, yes. Fifty guineas was bet on the outcome of a trotting match between Norwich and Watton in 1806, ten guineas was wagered on a match between two horses on the turnpike between Setch and King's Lynn in January 1801, while £20 (almost £1,400 in modern money) a side was ventured on a match run from Downham Market to Fincham. In 1840, a chestnut mare named Lady Jane was a winner at stakes of 100 guineas in a race against time held at Swaffham. No doubt plenty of unreported gambling was going on as well. Strange wagers could be made, not entirely related to the main event. At Swaffham Races, in September 1829, a Mr Farrer bet Mr Cooke that he would produce a pair of working oxen that could beat any pair of horses Cooke could produce to plough an acre of land. Horseracing continues to thrive in the eastern region, and is a great day out, notably at racecourses in Newmarket, Great Yarmouth, Fakenham and Huntingdon.

The last days of camping

It wasn't football. It wasn't rugby. Nor was it boxing. Well, not quite. Camping – or campball – was an early precursor of all three, incorporating elements of each. In East Anglia people had played the game since the Middle Ages, probably far earlier. By the 19th century it was a dying sport, but it did not go down without a fight.

Nothing to do with pitching tents, then?

Camping was a rough and tumble ball game, usually comprising 10-a-side teams, though squads of 24 players were not unknown. The game was particularly popular in Norfolk and Suffolk, before being eclipsed by other ball sports later in the 1800s. That said, as late as the 1820s, crowds of more than 6,000 would turn out for an eagerly anticipated match between local rivals. This was physically dangerous and, frankly, violent stuff. Not for the faint-hearted. According to one report, which has not been verified so needs treating with a little suspicion, up to nine men died as a result of injuries sustained in a camping match at Diss. For all that, there were rules, teams, goals and passing to team-mates by way of throwing the ball. This could either be the size of a cricket ball or a football, depending on where you were. There were also stand-up fist fights and wrestling that seemed to be an accepted part of the game.

Who can we blame for all this mayhem?

Nobody is sure quite how far back in time the game goes. Some say the Roman army brought it here. The Latin word 'campus' was initially used to denote an open space used for a sporting or martial enterprise, such as the Campus Martius (Field of Mars) in Rome. Perhaps Roman settlements in Norfolk and Suffolk created their own 'campus' area while this island was part of the empire? Certainly, by the Middle Ages, camping was one of the more violent sorts of folk football. Writer Thomas Tusser, in the 16th century, referred to it being played in meadows or pastures. Other observers say camping was part of communal rivalry, in which teams from either side of a town or village tried to score a goal in 'opposition' territory – and claim local bragging rights. This has modern echoes in the Shrove Tuesday games still played in places like Ashbourne, Derbyshire. Open ground, often near churches, was used for games. At Swaffham the area known as Campingland, was probably the pitch. Stiffkey has a 'Camping Hill', Colkirk has its 'Camping Land', as does Whissonsett. By the early 19th century these ancient folk matches were becoming rarer, but they still had life in them. In Norfolk, the village of Ranworth was the place to go for camping. On June 10, 1822, two teams of ten-a-side from Ranworth and neighbouring parishes matched up there. In front of 6,000 people, "after half an hour's excellent sport, which produced some good set-tos and a few bloody noses, victory was declared in favour of Ranworth", according to our ever-reliable Norfolk Annals. The following month, at the same venue, Blofield played against Tunstead and Happing Hundreds. After the game finished goalless, "Turner, of Witton, and Riches, of Upton, had a pugilistic trial of manhood. A well-fought battle of 32 rounds of hard milling ended in favour of Riches".

Did the result of the game matter?

It does sound as if the introduction of the ball was merely incidental to local lads enjoying a good ruckus. However, someone *was* keeping the score. There were plenty of prizes on offer, though local pride was surely the greatest motivation. In 1806 a match was announced at Crostwick Common, between Taverham and Blofield. Two teams of young men, who had to be under 25 and unmarried, were to do battle for a hat each, worth 10s 6d. In the event, despite a "vast concourse of spectators" turning up, the match was a walkover. Blofield failed to show up, for unspecified reasons. Some years later the Blofield men made amends in a 10-a-side game at Worstead against Tunstead and Happing. On this occasion sadly, "a poor old man who had repaired thither to see the sport fell down and expired on the spot". Whipping boys Blofield had another day to forget at Norwich Cricket Ground. They took on the city men, but "gave up", according to the rather jaundiced reporter of the Norfolk Chronicle. "Neither the camping nor the subsequent wrestling were well-contested," he added, with a verbal scowl. A few days before the Battle of Waterloo, in June, 1815, Ranworth once again hosted a "grand camping game" in front of 3,000 fans. "They played 24-a-side, but neither party goaled the ball, and it was decided by a bye."

Who watched these games?

Norfolk MP and Government minister William Windham, whose family owned Felbrigg Hall, near Cromer, was said to be a fan of these "ancient sports and amusements". He was spotted among the crowds at camping. In June, 1818, when Norfolk defeated Suffolk in a "spirited contest" held at Kirby Cane, among the thousands of spectators watching were "gentlemen of rank and fortune". But it seems likely most were ordinary people, sports lovers who might also take in a boxing match or horse race. As society became more orderly by the mid-19th century, sports followed suit. Boxing was governed by the Queensberry Rules, Rugby and Association football were fostered by the disciplined gentlemen formed by public schools. They grew in popularity. There was no place in Victorian England for the rude country cousin that was camping. Its last mention in the Norfolk Annals comes in a match held at Norwich Cricket Ground in 1831, and even then it was noted that the game had not been played there for nearly 20 years. The Norfolk-Suffolk contest at Kirby Cane in 1818 was said to be the first "thorough boxing camping match in the past 35 years". "Considering that not five out of the 20 individuals who played had ever before been engaged in any pugilistic contest, it was astonishing to observe the spirit of gallantry which animated both parties". Gallant certainly, but it was the end of an era. More polite ball games were here to stay. We can only imagine the reactions of those battered and bruised veterans of the camping tradition as it faded from history and into legend.

Weavers' woes

On June 12, 1827, the 12th Lancers charged into action in Norwich. They were not fighting a foreign army, but a group of angry workers. Norfolk's once proud weaving industry was sinking into decline, but it would not go quietly.

An industrial, but sometimes troubled, city

East Anglia, and Norwich in particular, had thrived on the cloth trade. Since medieval times, wool had been the country's greatest export. East Anglia's proximity to its chief customers – the trading ports of the Netherlands – put it in a good position. In Norwich and other Norfolk towns hand loom weavers seemed to be everywhere. Most of them were self-employed, working from home, often in top floor rooms with high ceilings to accommodate their tall looms. Many kept caged canaries for company while they worked, which must have given city streets a distinctive noise. Daniel Defoe, visiting Norwich in 1724, wrote: ". . . the inhabitants being all so busy at their manufactures, dwell in their garrets at their looms and in their combing-shops. . . almost all the works they are employed on being done within doors." Worsted weavers and cordwainers dominated the trade, with employers putting work out to individual artisans. These proud, independently-minded people provided the backbone of Norwich's economy – but they were vulnerable when periodic trade decline put them out of work. Wars were bad news, as their markets could be cut off by naval blockade. Nevertheless, the weavers thrived for much of the 18th century. Norwich was still England's second biggest city, and their top quality product was admired worldwide.

A large workforce?

Arthur Young, another astute visitor, reckoned in 1771 there were 12,000 looms in Norwich alone. This in a city which, by 1801, had a population of 36,000. But trouble lay ahead. In 1793 Britain went to war with revolutionary France. Closure of the seas hit trade. Unemployment soared. This slump proved longer lasting than most. Meanwhile, the rise of the industrial midlands and north was toppling Norwich as a manufacturing base. Factories and steam-powered machinery allowed the industrialists of Manchester and Leeds to undercut Norwich's high quality product, selling at greater volume and lower price. Norfolk could not compete. It was not until the 1830s that the city got its first mill. William Taylor, a member of one of the city's merchant dynasties, declared in 1812: "Norwich's sunset is arrived." Taylor, who preferred literature to labour, abandoned trade for his first love – translating German works. Weavers did not have that luxury. The death of Norfolk's weaving trade was long drawn out and tragic.

An inevitable death?

What appears unavoidable with hindsight is not always apparent to those dealing with the present. Attempts were made to avoid decline. In 1809, for example, the employers gathered in Norwich to raise wages; a few years later the East India Company increased its order for goods. But when the city lost its monopoly to supply that company – and that in China – it was another nail in the coffin. There was a welcome coup for the city in 1816 when the popular Princess Charlotte, daughter of the Prince Regent, announced she would wear and promote Norwich bombazines – quality silk fabric. The benefits of this 'celebrity endorsement' were lost the following year with the sudden death of the young princess. In 1822 wages were cut – a result of competition with Yorkshire manufacturers. Workers mobbed the employers, meeting at Norwich Guildhall, where a Mr William Bosley was "very roughly handled, and his hat, coat and shoes taken from him and torn to pieces". Although troops were called out, the employers relented. The weavers celebrated.

Round one to the workers

It was a losing battle. This industrial unrest coincided with a period of nationwide strife. Agricultural workers were also in uproar about introduction of machinery that hit wages and employment. The government reacted by banning trades unions and cracking down on dissent. Weavers attacked people wearing what they recognised as imported cloth. In 1826 the Norwich Court of Guardians raised several thousand pounds to support unemployed weavers, on condition the men agreed to a drop in wages. The weavers refused the offer. The following June it came to a head. A group of Wymondham weavers were arrested for damaging machinery at Ashwellthorpe. With the machine-breakers imprisoned in Norwich Castle, the authorities brought in witnesses in coaches guarded by troops of the 12th Lancers, based in the city. The Norwich weavers were ready to support their Wymondham brethren. They built barricades at the Golden Ball and Castle Bridge entrances to Castle Meadow, and threw stones at the cavalry. Reinforcements, accompanied by special constables, then charged the weavers and drove them off. A number of men subsequently stood trial, but Judge Baron Garrow, perhaps aware how delicate the situation was, dealt with them relatively leniently. David Secker, Henry Rix and William Thurston were accused of riotous assembly, which carried the death penalty. Their astute defence lawyer, a Mr Cooper, pointed out that although the Riot Act had been read to the crowd, the wording was slightly incorrect. On this technicality, the three were acquitted, the judge hoping they "would go home sensible of the blessings of Providence in having shielded them that day from an ignominious death". The Ashwellthorpe rioters were bound over to keep the peace in the sum of £50 each.

Round two to the law!
As trade deteriorated, there was more rioting. Intimidation of employers and attacks on machinery and materials continued. Two looms placed in a workhouse were destroyed by strikers, and a manufacturer named John Wright had vitriol thrown in his face in St Faith's Lane, causing terrible injuries. Richard Nockolds, later hanged for arson, admitted to the assault. In 1829 "many unemployed weavers

paraded the streets, headed by a muffled drum and a shuttle bound in crape". A meeting at the Guildhall led to the setting up of a relief fund for jobless men and their families. It soon raised £3,000, but trouble continued. Manufacturers accused of undercutting wages were targeted. Disguised men broke into the house of William Springhall, of St Augustine's, cut work from his looms and even fired a pistol at him. Similar violence broke out at Saxlingham, as feelings ran high. Troops of the 7th Dragoon Guards were called out to deter further attacks.

Who was speaking for the workers?
Radical agitator William Cobbett addressed workers at Ranelagh Gardens, Norwich, in 1830, on 'The State of the Country'. He was blamed by many for fanning unrest. Cobbett, never afraid of controversy, travelled the land protesting at the hardships of working people. In Norwich he was denounced by an opponent as "one who had crawled from the very dregs of the people to a slimy popularity". No doubt Cobbett gave as good as he got. A further strike in 1838 at a new factory built by a Mr Robberds saw the new police force protecting workers brought in by the factory owner. By that time it was estimated there were only 4,000 looms left in Norwich; in the north, which became the powerhouse of what was later known as the Industrial Revolution, some 750,000 were said to be at work. Some aspects of the trade continued in Norfolk, such as manufacture of quality silk shawls for a niche luxury market, but the glory days were over. Norwich, along with its canaries, had been toppled from its perch as England's second city. By 1845 it was described as "formerly a great manufacturing city, but declined of late". The mill at Whitefriars, which still stands, is one of the few reminders of these days.

Hard times. . .
It wasn't all doom and gloom. Unemployment was eased by the rise of the boot and shoe industry, as well as the growth of light engineering. As the 19th century came to an end, it was a very different looking and sounding Norwich that looked forward to a new age.

A grand farewell

In July, 1842, Norfolk said goodbye to a giant of the county. A man synonymous with Norfolk itself. Thomas William Coke.

Invented the Agricultural Revolution, didn't he?

Thomas William Coke, Earl of Leicester, will always be known as an agricultural improver. As noted earlier in the tale of Turnip Townshend, modern historians tend to downplay the role of individual pioneers, but he was an influential figure in the process that helped British farmers feed the country's growing population. The owner of the mighty Holkham estate, in north Norfolk, he was an improving farms landlord, a man who brought new ideas in livestock to the fore and turned poor quality land into a profitable estate. Above all, he was a proper Norfolk character. Coke spent his early life not in Norfolk, but Derbyshire. His father was Wenman Roberts, nephew of the builder of Holkham. Roberts' mother Anne had eloped with a Derbyshire man, and been estranged from the family. But when her son inherited the estate in 1775 he changed his name to Coke. His death within a year left his own 21-year-old son to inherit. Cutting short his Grand Tour of Europe, he came to Holkham. Coke's bid to improve the unprofitable farms there became a labour of love which lasted more than 30 years. Farming folk gathered at annual three-day meetings at Holkham at sheep-shearing time – the Holkham Clippings – from Britain and from overseas. He is credited with improvements to animal breeding and husbandry relating to cattle, sheep and pigs. He planted more than a million trees at Holkham and created the park there, still a haven for wildlife.

Popular chap?

Coke's Clippings were the fore-runners of today's agricultural shows, as much social occasions as farming ones. This helps explain Coke's popularity. He was esteemed throughout the county. Norwich-born

---

writer Harriet Martineau later remembered him as "my early ideal of the patriotic gentleman of England". For more than 50 years he was MP for Norfolk. He became known as 'Coke of Norfolk' to differentiate him from another Coke in Parliament, but the name seemed fitting. Norfolk people took him to their hearts. In politics he was a Whig, a friend of Charles James Fox. Politics were partisan then; his motto was "Never trust a Tory". For years he refused a peerage, content to be 'Mr Coke,' but accepted the Earldom of Leicester from the young Queen Victoria, insisting only that the title include the words 'of Holkham'. In the late 1830s he retired from public life. Then in his eighties, but still hale and hearty, he moved with his second wife, Anne, to Longford in Derbyshire. It was there he died on June 30, 1842, aged 88. The scene was set for the closest thing Norfolk has seen to a royal send-off.

Nothing like a grand exit. . .

After lying for two days in state at Longford, Coke began his final journey. He was to lie at Tittleshall, where his ancestor, the first great Coke of Norfolk, Chief Justice Edward Coke, the man who laid down the English Common Law in the 17th century, was buried. As the funeral cortege entered Norfolk, on July 7, it became clear how revered Coke was. Crowds lined roads, according to one contemporary, "amid deep silence, only interrupted by the tramp of horsemen, the grating of the carriage wheels and the heavy tolling of bells in the villages through which it passed." At King's Lynn the townspeople, from highest to most humble, wore mourning. Black flags flew from the gates, from buildings and from ships in the harbour. At the Crown Hotel his body lay overnight. Some 1,500 people filed past it, with 1,000 turned away. Next day the body was taken on to Swaffham. Attempts to keep the funeral as private as possible were thwarted by the sheer numbers of people wishing to pay their respects. On the eve of the funeral thousands made their way to line the route. Country people in waggons and carts parked at every conceivable point on the route, many sleeping in them, or in the fields, camped on mattresses or wrapped in cloaks amid the hay.

Hoping for good weather, no doubt!

The morning of Monday, July 11, dawned bright and clear. Many said the gathering reminded them of Coke's sheep shearings; the same time of the year, the summer weather. Now an extraordinary scene unfolded. The official funeral procession was led by the Holkham steward, with 150 estate tenants on horseback. Carriages followed, with pall bearers and clergy. Coke's hearse was drawn by six horses, the coffin draped in a crimson pall. Behind it came a long train of coaches carrying friends and relatives, 200 gentlemen on horseback and more vehicles containing neighbours, tenants and yeomen farmers. At its outset it was two miles long, and more people joined it en route. At Lexham, for example, more than 150 horsemen tagged along. Even more watched it pass, with up to 15,000 in Swaffham queuing overnight for the privilege. Finally the massive procession reached the little Church of St Mary at Tittleshall, 15 miles south of Holkham. Much of the land there was owned by the Coke family. Coke of Norfolk was laid to rest in the mausoleum of his ancestors, amid the memorials to former Cokes. He was the last of the family to be buried there. Most poignant perhaps was the tomb of Jane, Coke's first wife. Built in 1805 and carved in white marble, it shows Jane being carried to heaven by an angel. The tomb was carved by Joseph Nollekens, the most fashionable portrait sculptor of his day, a favourite of King George III.

Anything else?

A little over three years later, in August 1845, another vast crowd turned out to view the postscript to Coke's life. An imposing monument reflecting his agricultural exploits, illustrated by depictions of farm animals, was unveiled in the grounds of Holkham. Lord Coborne laid the foundation stone, watched by "a large gathering of the nobility and gentry and of the tenant farmers of Norfolk". This monument still stands today. Originally the plan was to put up a similar display at Castle Hill, Norwich, but it was only fitting it should stand where Coke had planted his lasting legacy – on the soil of north Norfolk.

A sensational murder

In April, 1849 a crowd estimated at more than 20,000 people turned out in Norwich. In a carnival atmosphere they were there to see one of the most infamous murderers of Victorian Norfolk hanged.

Well, it's a day out. . .

Public executions were treated by many as a form of entertainment, much to the distress of the authorities. But the interest created by double killer James Blomfield Rush spread beyond Norfolk. The killing of the distinguished Isaac Jermy, Recorder of Norwich and president of Norwich Union, and his son at Stanfield Hall, near Wymondham, set pulses racing. The story reads like a thriller, full of sub-plots. It begins in 1800 when farmer's daughter Mary Blomfield, of Tacolneston, gave birth to an illegitimate son, James. It seems the father was a "gentleman resident in Wymondham" who had promised to marry Mary, but deserted her. She eventually married farmer John Rush two years later, who allowed young James to use his surname. Educated at grammar school in Eye, Suffolk, he set up as a tenant farmer in Aylsham, aged 24. He seemed to be on the straight and narrow when he married Susannah Soames four years later; the couple went on to have nine children in the next 12 years.

Very normal. . .

All was not well. Rush was in financial difficulties. Money, or the lack thereof, seems to have been at the root of his subsequent behaviour. That and a vicious property dispute. The mysterious deaths of his stepfather in 1844 and his mother four years later raised questions locally, as did a codicil added to his stepfather's will which left his estate to Rush instead of his children, as was originally intended. Rush senior had died as a result of a shotgun incident, and Mary Rush's death was suspected to be by poison. After Susannah died, the situation became more complicated. Rush hired Emily Sandford as a governess to his children, but the two became lovers, and she expected him to marry her. Things came to a head when Rush fell out with his landlords, the Jermys. They had come into possession of Stanfield Hall close to Rush's property, Potash Farm. Isaac Jermy and his son Isaac Jermy Jermy (the names are confusing as they had changed their surname from Preston as a result of a family dispute) held Rush's future in their hands. Relations between Rush and his new landlords deteriorated as it became clear the mortgage on Potash Farm was about to be foreclosed on November 30, 1848. To keep the pot boiling, Rush was on friendly terms with rival claimants for the property, Thomas Jermy and John Larner, who had tried to get hold of Stanfield Hall. Two days before the mortgage deadline, only the death of Isaac Jermy would keep a roof over Rush's head. Witnesses later said he had threatened them.

The classic motive?

On the evening of November 28, 1848 Isaac Jermy stepped outside during a game of cards with his family. A butler later reported hearing a shot, and Jermy junior went outside to investigate. After a further shot his wife Sophia and the housemaid, Elizabeth Chestney, rushed outside. They found father and son shot at point blank range. Both women were also shot, and wounded – but survived. The servants later described a cloaked man with a pistol pursuing the women. A groom ran three miles to the police station at Wymondham, where a telegraph to Norwich summoned reinforcements, who were sent in carriages. As Rush was suspected, they surrounded his house and arrested him in the early hours of the next morning. He had an alibi ready; Emily Sandford initially testified he had been out of the house a matter of minutes. The police were having none of it; both were arrested, and Rush was charged with murder after being identified by Mrs Jermy and the servants. The murders caused a sensation. Victorian Britain loved a good, juicy murder, and this appealed to everyone. The popular newspapers had a field day, and even Charles Dickens came up to Norfolk to take a look at the murder scene. Rush's trial opened on March 29 the following year at the Norfolk Assizes in Norwich, and lasted a week. In front of a packed public gallery he defended himself, eventually on his feet for a total of 14 hours. His cross-examining of Emily Sandford, who withdrew her alibi, went horribly wrong. She spent a total of nine-and-a-half hours in the witness box over two days, most of them being grilled by Rush himself. "It was full of repetitions, and everything material might have been said in a tithe of the time," reported a contemporary chronicler. It served only to contradict his claims of innocence. Mrs Jermy and the housemaid gave evidence against him, the latter having to be brought in a special chair as she had not recovered from her wounds. After that, the judge, Mr Baron Rolfe, summed up, the jury consulted for a few minutes, before bringing in a verdict of guilty. Rush was sentenced to death.

Can't beat a good hanging!

Sentence was carried out on April 21, by which time public interest peaked. Cheap return tickets were issued in London for Norwich, and thousands arrived at the railway station, which had only been opened five years earlier. Police boarded the trains at Attleborough, turning off known pickpockets intent on working the crowds. Such was the enthusiasm to see the hanging, "one woman who had been confined only three weeks before travelled from the country on foot fourteen miles". Rush was hanged at noon on Castle Hill. To the end he displayed a cool arrogance, even prompting Calcraft, the executioner, to "put the knot a little higher up, don't hurry". A reporter wrote: "The greatest silence prevailed, the solemn stillness being only broken by the solitary shriek of a woman who had fainted in the crowd."

Did he think he could get away with it?

His behaviour in court indicated it, but a posthumous examination of his skull showed it was characterised by acquisition, aggression and self-esteem. His "reflective organs were exceedingly small", wrote a phrenologist. Rush was an impulsive and violent man. Emily Sandford was released, and went to live in Australia.

Select bibliography

Like all writers I owe a huge debt to a variety of primary and secondary sources. Below is a list of some of them.

The Anglo-Saxon Chronicles – anon

Ecclesiastical History of the English People – Bede

Folk Heroes of Britain – Charles Kightly

Folk Tales of the British Isles – Kevin Crossley-Holland

Collected Ghost Stories – M R James

In Search of the Dark Ages – Michael Wood

1066 The Year of the Three Battles, Frank McLynn, 1998

Saint Wendreda, March, Trevor Bevis

English Heritage Book of Norwich, Brian Ayers, 1994

A History of Norwich – Frank Meeres

Medieval Norwich – ed Carole Rawcliffe and Richard Wilson

The King's War – C V Wedgwood

God's Englishman – Christopher Hill

Free-Born John – Pauline Gregg

Religion and the Decline of Magic – Keith Thomas

The Stripping of the Altars – Eamon Duffy

Britain and the World (1649-1815) – J R Jones

A History of Britain – Simon Schama

The Ascent of Money – Niall Ferguson

Norfolk Portraits, Norfolk Gallery and Norfolk in the Civil War – R W Ketton-Cremer

Diary of a Country Parson – James Woodforde

Norfolk Annals 1801-1850 – Charles Mackie

The Buildings of England – Nikolaus Pevsner and Bill Wilson

The Making of the English Working Class – E P Thompson

Oxford Dictionary of National Biography

The Norwich Knowledge – Michael Loveday

Also by **Peter Sargent**

A Moment in Time

50 stories that bring East Anglian history to life.

ISBN 9780995618718, published October 2017, price £12

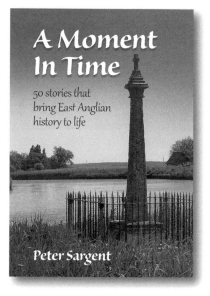

In this series of short stories, encounter famous figures who made their mark on the eastern counties. You'll also meet less familiar figures and veer off the beaten track. Here are tales of a Cambridgeshire Iron Age 'hill fort', Norfolk's raffish 19th Century bare knuckle boxers and the sailors who fought a huge, but barely remembered, 17th century sea battle off the Suffolk coast.

"Peter Sargent has gathered together 50 stories from our past for a brilliant new book... A Moment in Time is a book that readers will want to dip into time and again to discover and rediscover the people and places that have helped shape our story."
Let's Talk Magazine

Keep up with Peter at www.petersargent.co.uk

A Place in History

50 more East Anglian moments in time

ISBN 978-0-9956187-6-3, published September 2018, price £12

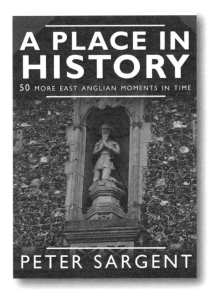

So many people have their place in history. For some it is a large and well-known slot, familiar to people in the present day. Others have a far more humble location, and are less well remembered. They all find their place in this book. Join author Peter Sargent on a 2,000-year journey through East Anglia's colourful and varied history.

"A glorious stroll through the life and times of not just Norwich and Norfolk, but the whole of East Anglia."
Derek James, Eastern Daily Press

Books and blogs at www.petersargent.co.uk

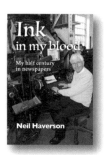

Paul Dickson Books

Books by Norfolk writers published in Norwich

Paul has lived and worked in Norfolk for the past 30 years, initially for the National Trust and, for the last 20 years, as an independent PR practitioner and latterly as an independent publisher and tour guide.

A meeting with Illuminée Nganemariya in 2006 saw Paul assisting with Miracle in Kigali, Illuminée's story of survival during the Rwandan Genocide and subsequent life in Norwich.

After a spell as a director of Norfolk's Tagman Press, Paul decided to branch out on his own. Since then he has embarked on collaborations with Norfolk writers Tony Ashman, Sandra Derry, Neil Haverson and Peter Sargent.

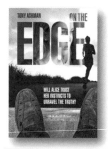

www.pauldicksonbooks.co.uk